Janice VanCleave's

Geography for Every Kid

Other Titles of Interest from Wiley

Science for Every Kid series:
Janice VanCleave's Astronomy for Every Kid
Janice VanCleave's Biology for Every Kid
Janice VanCleave's Chemistry for Every Kid
Janice VanCleave's Earth Science for Every Kid
Janice VanCleave's Math for Every Kid
Janice VanCleave's Physics for Every Kid

Spectacular Science Projects series:
Janice VanCleave's Animals
Janice VanCleave's Earthquakes
Janice VanCleave's Gravity
Janice VanCleave's Machines
Janice VanCleave's Magnets
Janice VanCleave's Microscopes and Magnifying Lenses
Janice VanCleave's Molecules

Flying Start Science series:
Action
Flight
Light
Pattern
Structure
Water

David Suzuki's Looking At series:
Looking at the Body
Looking at the Environment
Looking at Insects
Looking at Plants
Looking at Senses
Looking at Weather

The Complete Handbook of Science Fair Projects, Julianne Bochinski

The Thomas Edison Book of Easy and Incredible Experiments, The Thomas Alva Edison Foundation

Janice VanCleave's

Geography for Every Kid

Easy Activities that Make Learning Geography Fun

John Wiley & Sons, Inc.

New York • Chichester • Brisbane • Toronto • Singapore

This text is printed on acid-free paper.

The publisher and the author have made every reasonable effort to insure that the
experiments and activities in this book are safe when conducted as instructed but
assume no responsibility for any damage caused or sustained while performing
the experiments or activities in this book. Parents, guardians, and/or teachers
should supervise young readers who undertake the experiments and activities in
this book.

Library of Congress Cataloging-in-Publication Data

VanCleave, Janice
    [Geography for every kid]
    Janice VanCleave's geography for every kid : easy activities that make
learning geography fun.
        p.   cm.
    Includes index.
    Summary: Introduces basic concepts of geography through simple
problems and activities such as constructing a clay map, making a
compass rose, and plotting the track of a hurricane.
    ISBN 0-471-59841-0 (acid-free). — ISBN 0-471-59842-9 (pbk. : acid-
free)
    1. Geography—Juvenile literature. [1. Geography.] I. Title.
G175.V36   1993
910—dc20   93-13305

Printed in the United States of America

10 9 8 7 6 5

This book is dedicated to a group of future world travelers, my grandchildren:

Kimberly, Jennifer, and Davin VanCleave
Lauren and Lacey Russell

Acknowledgments

I want to thank a group of children from First Baptist Church of Marlin, Texas, who met weekly to eagerly help me test and refine a number of the procedures and exercises. We worked together to ensure that only fully tested, workable problems were included. Part of their greatest contribution was their enthusiastic reaction to the activities. Thank you: Will Butler, Brinson Bryan, Jeffrey Drake, Scott Drake, Jarrod Hogg, Brett Patrick Jenkins, Matthew Jennings, Nathan Jennings, and Will Johnson.

Contents

Introduction

This is a basic geography book designed to teach facts, concepts, and problem-solving strategies. Geography is a part of our daily lives; each section introduces geographical concepts in a way that makes learning useful and fun.

Geography is a branch of science that encompasses all aspects of the earth's physical features and inhabitants. It is the study of almost anything about the earth—the distribution of its people, animals, and plants; land, sea, and air features; weather conditions—the list can seem endless. The difference between the study of geography and other sciences is that geography examines its subjects from a perspective of where they are located and what relationship they have with the things around them. Other sciences tend to focus on subjects individually.

This book concentrates on teaching map skills, climate regions and weather patterns, land and water masses, and population distribution. A foundation of basic geography facts is essential for everyone. Questions such as Where? How far? or How do you get there? are part of everyday living. Understanding geography can help you find the answers to such questions by providing the skills needed to read maps and globes. This book will make you more comfortable with geography concepts and provide a few basic tools to lead you to make more geographic discoveries on your own.

Maps have been important to humans for a long time. The first maps were drawn in the dirt by prehistoric travelers, who recognized the importance of sharing their knowledge about the location of places and things. These first dirt maps were crudely drawn with a stick on the ground and were not portable. Today, globes and maps are available to provide school children with detailed information about places right down the street or around the world.

Has all information about geography been uncovered and recorded? No. Geography is a living, growing science. With the improvement of mapmaking tools and means of transportation, today's geographers can study and chart not only the lands on earth, but also those on other celestial bodies.

This book presents geographical information in a way that you can easily understand and use. The problems, experiments, and other activities were selected for their ability to explain concepts with little complexity. One of the main objectives is to present the fun that can be had with geography.

Read each of the 20 sections slowly and follow all procedures carefully. You will learn best if each section is read in order, as there is some buildup of information as the book progresses. The format for each section is:

1. What You Need to Know: Background information and an explanation of terms.

2. Let's Think It Through: Questions to be answered or situations to be solved using the information from What You Need to Know.

3. Answers: Step-by-step instructions for solving the questions posed in Let's Think It Through.

4. Exercises: Practice problems to reinforce your skills.

5. Activity: A project to allow you to apply the skill to a problem-solving situation in the real world.

6. Solutions to Exercises: Step-by-step instructions for solving the Exercises.

7. Glossary: All **bold-faced** terms are defined in a Glossary at the end of the book. Be sure to flip back to the Glossary

as often as necessary, making each term part of your personal vocabulary.

8. Some sections also include a Geographer's Toolbox with step-by-step instructions for making tools to use in the section.

General Instructions for *Let's Think It Through* and *Exercise* Sections

1. Study each question carefully by reading through it once or twice, then follow the steps described in the Answers.

2. Do the same thing for the Exercises, following the steps described in the Answers to the *Let's Think It Through* questions.

3. Check your answers to evaluate your work.

4. Do the work again if any of your answers are incorrect.

General Instructions for *Activity* Sections

1. Read the Activity completely before starting.

2. Collect the supplies. You will have less frustration and more fun if all the necessary materials for the activity are ready before you start. You lose your train of thought when you have to stop and search for supplies.

3. Do not rush through the Activity. Follow each step very carefully; never skip steps, and do not add your own. Safety is of utmost importance, and by reading each Activity before starting, and then following the instructions exactly, you can feel confident that no unexpected results will occur.

4. Observe. If your results are not the same as those described in the Activity, carefully reread the instructions, and start over from step 1.

1

The Earth in Space

Study and Interpret Past and Present Models of the Solar System

What You Need to Know

The early Greek **astronomers** (people who study the stars and other objects in space) tried to figure the distance from the earth to the sun and the moon. Without the aid of a telescope, these scientists mapped the universe, placing the earth in the center and the stars, moon, and sun moving around it. To explain the movements of the celestial bodies, they described the sky as a huge hollow ball surrounding the earth. The stars, moon, and sun were located on the inside of the ball, and as the ball turned, so moved the stars, moon, and sun in the sky. As time passed, the models could not explain why some celestial bodies seemed to wander across the heavens. The astronomers called these bodies **planets** (the Greek word for wanderer).

In about A.D. 140, the Greek astronomer Ptolemy suggested a model of the universe that placed the planets, moon, and sun in revolving paths around the earth. His model also showed that the planets moved in small circles as they traveled along these paths. It was not until 1543 that a Polish astronomer, Nicholas Copernicus, proposed a model that placed the sun in the center and the planets, including the earth, revolving around it. Both models are shown on the following pages.

PTOLEMY'S MODEL

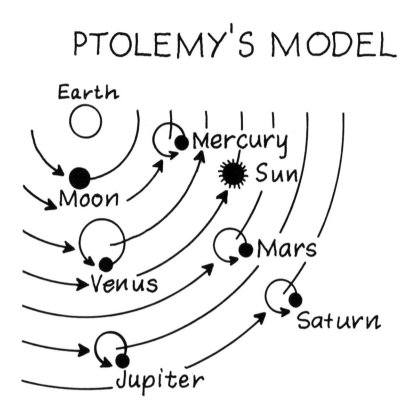

Let's Think It Through

Compare the models of the universe proposed by Ptolemy and Copernicus to answer the following questions.

1. Which model best describes a **solar system** (a group of celestial bodies traveling around a sun)?

2. How is the position of the earth different in each model?

3. How many planets were known at the time of Ptolemy and Copernicus?

COPERNICUS'S MODEL

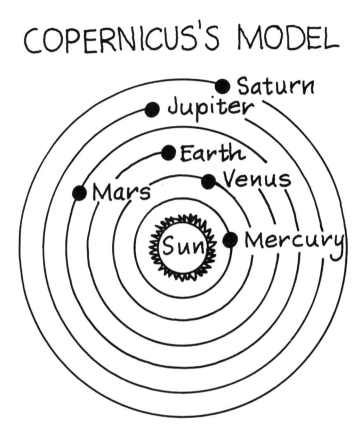

Answers

Think!

1. Copernicus's model describes a solar system which has the sun as its center and planets traveling around it.

2. In Ptolemy's model, the earth is the center of the system. But in Copernicus's model, the earth is the third planet out from the sun.

3. Six planets were known at the time of both astronomers. The planets were Mercury, Venus, Earth, Mars, Jupiter, and Saturn.

Exercises

Use the modern model of the solar system to answer the following questions.

1. How many planets are known today?

2. Does the modern map indicate that the position of the earth has changed from that proposed by Copernicus?

MODERN MODEL

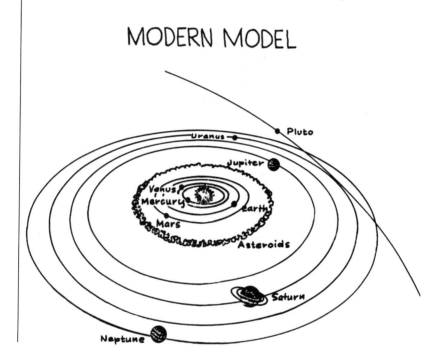

Activity: PATHWAYS

Purpose To demonstrate the path of the planets Mercury, Venus, Earth, and Mars around the sun.

Materials scissors
ruler
string
poster board, 18 inches (45 cm) square
cardboard, 18 inches (45 cm) square
pencil
2 pushpins

Procedure

1. Cut a 24-inch (60-cm) piece of string.

2. Fold the string in half.

3. Tie the folded string into a knot to form a loop that is about 6 inches (15 cm) long.

4. Tie a second knot in the remaining string that is about 1 inch (2.5 cm) below the first knot.

5. Tie a third knot about 1 inch (2.5 cm) below the second knot.

6. Tie a fourth knot about 1 inch (2.5 cm) below the third knot.

7. Lay the poster board on top of the cardboard.

8. In the center of the poster board, draw a line 5 inches (13 cm) long and stick a pushpin at each end of the line.

9. Position the 6-inch (15-cm) loop of string around the pushpins.

10. Place the pencil so that its point is against the inside of the loop.

11. Keep the string taut as you guide the pencil around the inside of the string to draw an elliptical path on the poster board.

12. Move the pencil inside the loop between the first and second knots and repeat the procedure.

13. Repeat the procedure between the second and third knots, and then between the third and fourth knots.

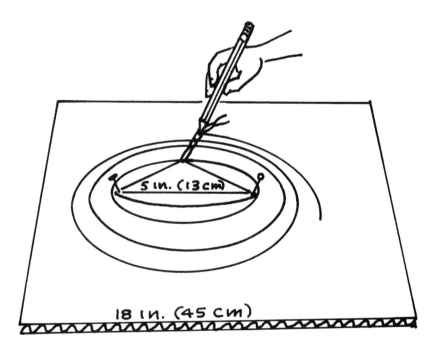

14. Remove the pushpins and draw a circle around a hole left by one of the push pins to represent the sun.

15. Draw one small circle on each elliptical path and label them Mercury, Venus, Earth, and Mars as indicated on the diagram.

THE EARTH IN SPACE

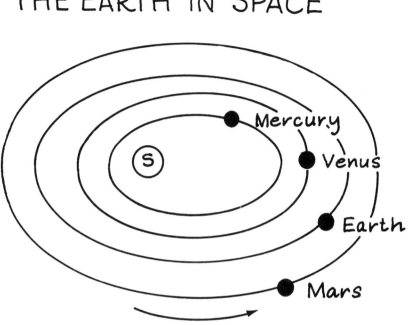

Results The elliptical paths of the four closest planets to the sun are drawn.

Why? The German astronomer Johannes Kepler (1571–1630) realized that the planets did not move in circular **orbits** (paths around the sun). Instead, the orbits were elliptical or egg shaped, with the sun being much closer to one end than the other. The speed of each planet varies during its elliptical orbit, being fastest when the planet is closest to the sun. As viewed from Polaris (the North Star), the planets move around the sun in a counterclockwise direction.

Solutions to Exercises

1. There are nine known planets: Mercury, Venus, Earth, Mars, Jupiter, Saturn, Uranus, Neptune, and Pluto.

2. No, the earth is the third planet from the sun on both models.

2
The History of Mapmaking

How to Use Ancient Mapping Symbols and Techniques

What You Need to Know

The first maps were drawings in the dirt. Although these ancient maps were crude, they were useful for directing people to food and water supplies and back to the safety of their homes, which may have been tents, huts, or caves. Symbols were used to indicate the location of geographic features along the route. Although they were instructive, the maps were not very practical. Because the map had to be left behind in the dirt, the travelers could only take a mental picture of its information with them.

As time passed, more permanent maps were made. People in every part of the world used local material in their mapmaking. Some people scratched maps onto damp clay that dried rock-hard in the sun. The Chinese painted maps on silk cloth, and Eskimos carved tiny wooden maps in driftwood. The notches in the wood showed the location of capes and bays. Polynesian islanders used a creative style known as a stick map, which was made by weaving reeds to show the direction to desired fishing spots. Seashells were attached to indicate the location of islands. Today, most **cartographers** (mapmakers) use paper to make maps.

Let's Think It Through

Og, the caveman, has drawn a map in the dirt for his wife, Iggle. The map directs Iggle to a nest of a large bird's eggs. Use the map to describe the directions that Og has given Iggle.

Answers

Think!

1. Walk from the cave toward the river.

2. Follow the path along the river toward the rising sun.

3. Turn away from the river when you reach the trees.

4. At the base of the mountain, look for a nest with a large, sleeping bird.

5. Put an egg in your basket and run home.

Og's Map

🄰 Cave

⋔ Mountains

_ _ _ Walk

_ . _ Run

♀ Tree

☼↑ Rising sun

〰 River

🐦 Sleeping bird

Exercise

Use Running Bear's map symbols and his directions below to draw a map that will direct his friend, Silver Fox, to an area where the young Indian brave can find deer.

Running Bear's Directions:

1. Place your canoe in the river that runs beside your home.

2. Travel the river for three days.

3. Leave the river and walk toward the rising sun.

4. The deer are in the mountains.

RUNNING BEAR'S MAP SYMBOLS

Mountains
Deer
River
Canoe
Rising Sun
Moon
Home
Silver Fox

Activity: CLAY MAPS

Purpose   To construct a clay map replica of ancient Babylonian clay tablets.

Materials   mixing bowl
spoon
2 cups (500 ml) table salt
1 cup (250 ml) flour
¾ cup (188 ml) tap water
eyedropper
3 drops of cooking oil
disposable aluminum pie pan
pencil
oven (optional)
adult helper (optional if not using oven)

Procedure

1. Make a batch of clay by following the steps below:
   - In the bowl, mix together the salt and flour.
   - Slowly add the water as you stir.
   - Use the eyedropper to add the oil. Stir.
2. Place the pie pan on a table.
3. Transfer the clay from the bowl to the pan.
4. Press against the clay with your hands to flatten and smooth its surface.
5. Use the point of the pencil to draw a map on the flat surface of the clay.

6. Place the pan with the clay tablet in the sun to dry, or ask an adult to bake it in an oven at a low heat of about 200°F (93°C) for one hour.

Results A hard, white clay tablet with map symbols is produced.

Why? Clay maps made in the desert kingdom of Babylonia are the oldest existing maps. These rocklike maps were drawn in soft clay in much the same way as you made your clay map. The Babylonian maps were dried by the heat from the sun (you may have chosen to use heat from an oven).

Solution to Exercise

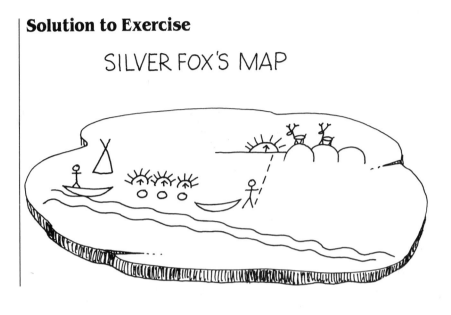

SILVER FOX'S MAP

3

Explorers

How Early Explorers Used Maps and the Stars to Determine Distance and Geographic Location

What You Need to Know

Long before European explorers bravely set sail to find new trade routes, people had strange ideas about the shape of the earth. Not knowing yet that it is a **sphere** (an object shaped like a ball), they imagined it as being a cube, a cone, a cylinder, a many-sided figure, a spiral, an island floating on endless water, or a flat plain beneath a round dome.

People have always been curious about what lies over the mountains or beyond the seas, but until the 1200s, few ventured very far from home. It wasn't until the late 1400s that explorations were made into the Atlantic Ocean, or what at that time was called the "Sea of Darkness." It is not hard to understand why these sailors might have been afraid to explore waters that were believed to be the home of giant monsters that pulled ships into the watery depths and ate the people on board.

Early European explorers sailed boldly into the unknown just as astronauts now chart courses through space. Explorers often gamble their lives to discover the unknown. Some lose the gamble, but others succeed. With each success, ideas about the world we live in change and information about geography increases.

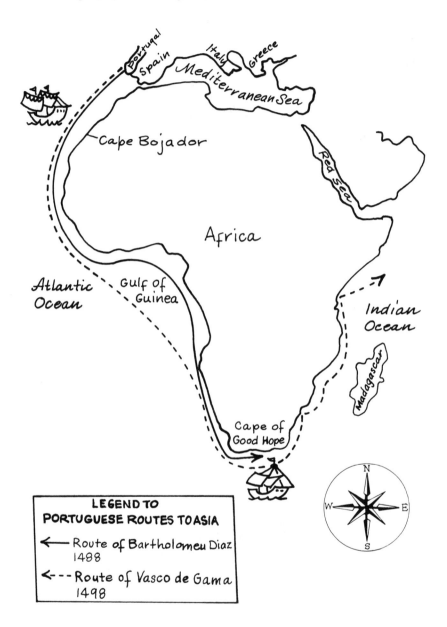

LEGEND TO
PORTUGUESE ROUTES TO ASIA

← Route of Bartholomeu Diaz
1488

←--- Route of Vasco de Gama
1498

Let's Think It Through

In the 1400s Prince Henry of Portugal believed it possible to reach Asia by sailing around Africa. He sent out ships, but his sailors refused to go much farther south than Cape Bojador, because it was believed that man-eating monsters waited on the nearby rocks for passing ships.

Use the map of the Portuguese routes to Asia to answer the following questions.

1. Which sea captain was the first to sail past the threatening rocks of Cape Bojador?

2. Where is the Cape of Good Hope?

Answers

1. *Think!*

- Which of the two route symbols in the legend has the earliest date?

- Find the symbol for that route in the legend. Who's route is it?

Bartholomeu Diaz was the first to sail past Cape Bojador, in 1488.

2. *Think!*

- Find the name Cape of Good Hope printed on the map.

- What is its location (upper, middle, lower)?

- What is the name of the section of land that it is printed on?

Cape of Good Hope is found at the lowest tip of Africa.

Exercises

In 1492 Columbus used maps prepared by the Greek geographer Ptolemy (A.D. 87–150), which showed the earth's circumference as 7,000 miles smaller than we now know it to be. Believing the earth to be round, he sailed westward in hopes of discovering a shorter route to the Spice Islands of India. Use the map showing the route of his journey to answer the following questions.

1. In what country did Columbus's voyage begin?

2. Where did he land after crossing the Atlantic Ocean?

Activity: STAR GAZING

Purpose To use the position of the star Polaris to determine the latitude of your home.

Materials scissors
ruler
string
2 pencils
paper hole-punch
24-by-14-inch (60-by-35-cm) poster board
marking pen
protractor
helper
masking tape

Procedure

NOTE: Steps 5–9 of this activity must be performed outdoors on a clear, moonless night.

1. Draw a half-circle on the edge of the poster board by following these steps:

   - Cut an 18-inch (45-cm) piece of string.

   - Tie one end of the string around one of the pencils.

   - Use the hole-punch to make a hole at the midpoint of one long edge of the poster board.

   - Stand the first pencil (with the string) in the center of the hole with the eraser end down. Stand a second pencil 12 inches (30 cm) away with the point down. Have your helper hold both pencils upright while you loosely tie the other end of the string to it so that the string between the two pencils is 12 inches (30 cm) long.

   - Hold the first pencil in the hole while you pull the second pencil until the string is taut.

- Keeping the string taut, move the point of the second pencil across the poster board until a half-circle is drawn.

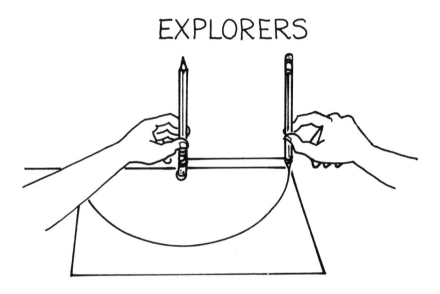

EXPLORERS

2. Cut out the paper half-circle.

3. Use the pen to label "N" (north), "S" (south), and "zenith," as shown in the diagram.

4. Cut a second 18-inch (45-cm) piece of string and tie it through the hole in the paper half-circle. Place a piece of tape across the hole.

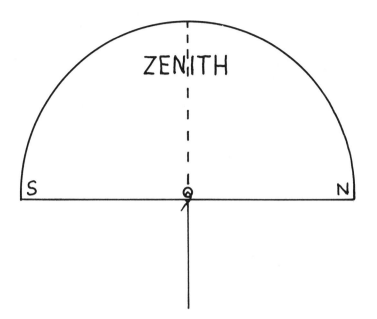

5. Stand outside and hold the paper half-circle against the side of your face so that its flat edge is level with your eyes, the zenith (top) of the half-circle points upward, and the north end is in front.

6. Hold the end of the string with one hand and pull it out to the north edge of the half-circle.

7. Turn your body until you locate the stars in the sky that form the Big Dipper constellation. Line up the two outermost stars in the bowl of the Big Dipper. Polaris (the North Star) is directly ahead.

8. Close one eye and use the other to line up the string with Polaris.

9. Ask your helper to mark a dot on the outer edge of the half-circle where the string crosses it.

10. Use a protractor and the dot to determine the angle of Polaris in the sky above you. Information on using a protractor can be found on pages 176–183 of *Math for Every Kid* (New York: Wiley, 1991) by Janice VanCleave.

Results   The angle of Polaris above the horizon varies depending on where you live.

Why?   The angle of **Polaris**, better known as the North Star, above the horizon is the same as the latitude of the observer. (Latitude is explained in the next chapter.) In the diagram, Polaris is in the northern sky about 33 degrees above the horizon, which is where Polaris appears to the observer who lives at 33 degrees north latitude (33°N). Should the person move to 40 degrees north latitude (40°N), Polaris could be seen in the northern sky 40 degrees above the horizon. Early explorers used the **altitude** (height) of Polaris above the horizon to navigate.

Solutions to Exercises

1. *Think!*

- The arrow indicates the direction of Columbus's route. What is the name of the country at the tail, or beginning, of the arrow?

Columbus began his trip in Spain.

2. *Think!*

- What is the name of the island and the name of the group of islands at the head, or end, of the arrow?

Columbus landed at San Salvador in the West Indies.

4
Global Addresses
Use Latitude and Longitude to Find Locations on a World Map

What You Need to Know

Cartographers use lines on their maps and globes to help locate places on the earth. These lines are called **latitude** and **longitude** lines. These lines are not on the real earth, but are imaginary lines that make using the globe or map easier. The lines circling the globe in an east-west direction are called **parallels of latitude** because the distance between any two latitude lines is always the same. The **equator** is the latitude line midway between the North and South poles as shown on page 32. It is the starting point, or zero degrees latitude (0°), for measuring distances in degrees north or south of the equator.

The lines circling the globe in a north-south direction are called **meridians of longitude**. Greenwich, England (near London), was selected as zero degrees longitude (0°), or the **prime meridian**, because it was the site of the most prominent astronomical observatory of its period. The prime meridian runs from the North Pole to the South Pole through Greenwich, and is the starting point for measuring distances in degrees east (right) or west (left).

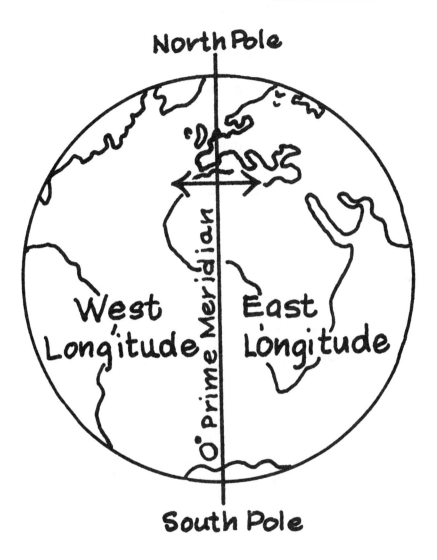

Lines of longitude and latitude crisscross to form a grid (equally spaced horizontal and vertical lines). Each line is labeled with its degree and direction and is called a **coordinate**. Providing the coordinates for the point where the latitude and longitude lines cross is like giving the address of that location. Every place on the globe has its own unique address. The diagram shows the address having the coordinates 29°N, 81°W.

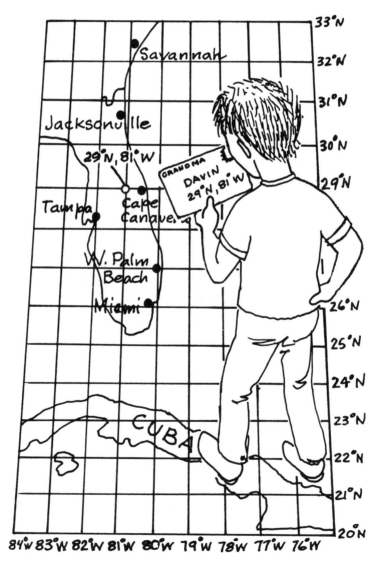

Let's Think It Through

Use the latitude and longitude maps to answer the following questions:

1. What is the latitude coordinate for the equator?

2. Through which landmass does latitude 60°N pass?

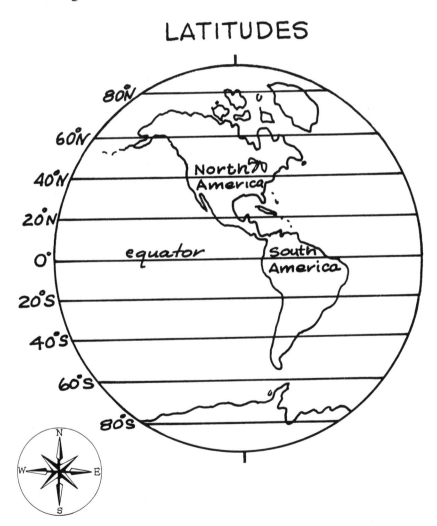

LATITUDES

3. Which longitude coordinates pass through Australia?

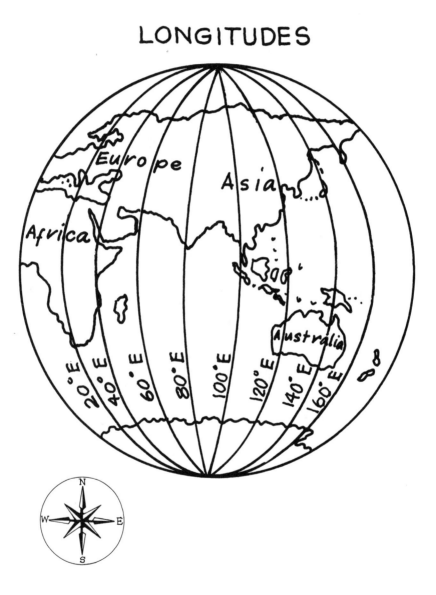

LONGITUDES

Answers

1. *Think!*

- What is the number of the latitude line labeled equator?

Zero.

- Does this latitude have a North or South direction?

No. Zero degrees (0°) is the latitude coordinate for the equator.

2. *Think!*

- Where is 60°N? There are two 60° lines on the map, one north (above) and one south (below) of the equator. N in the coordinate indicates that it is the latitude line above the equator on the map.

Latitude 60°N passes through the continent of North America.

3. *Think!*

- Find Australia on the map. How many longitude lines pass through the continent?

Two. The longitude coordinates 120°E and 140°E pass through Australia.

Exercises

Use the map to identify the countries where you find each of the following coordinates:

1. 40°N, 5°W

2. 45°N, 25°E

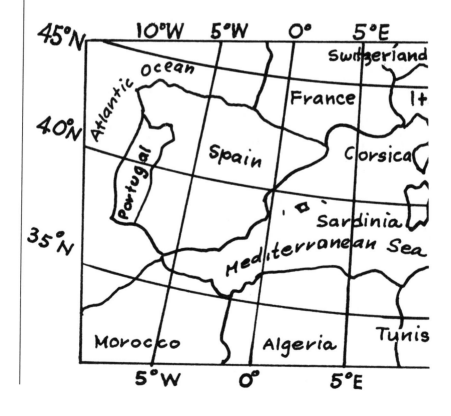

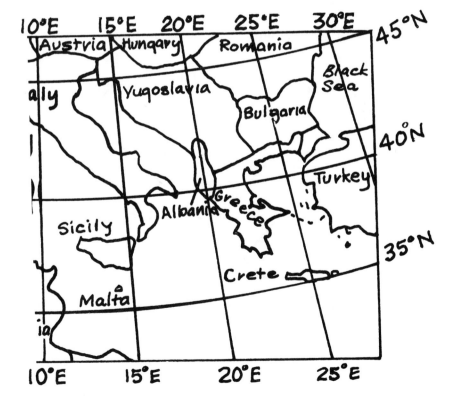

Activity: FATTER AND FATTER

Purpose To determine why there is a difference between the circumference of the earth between the equator and the North and South Poles.

Materials scissors
ruler
construction paper, 16 inch (40 cm) long
glue stick
paper hole-punch
pencil

Procedure

1. Cut two strips of paper each 2 inches × 16 inches (5 cm × 40 cm).

2. Glue the strips together at their centers to form an X.

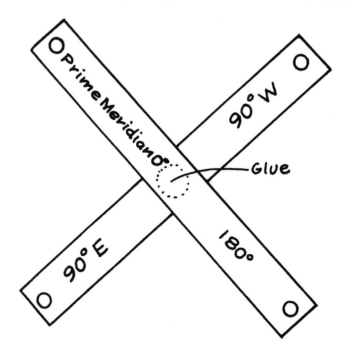

3. Label one strip "Prime Meridian 0°" and "180°" and the other "90°E" and "90°W" as indicated in the diagram.

4. Bring the four ends together so that they overlap, and glue them together to form a sphere.

5. Allow the glue to dry.

6. Use the hole-punch to punch a hole through the center of the overlapped ends.

7. Push the pencil through until the strips are about 2 inches (5 cm) above the point.

8. Hold the pencil between your palms with the paper strips below, and imagine a horizontal line around the widest circumference of the strips.

9. Move your hands back and forth to make the paper strips spin and observe how the distance between the strips changes.

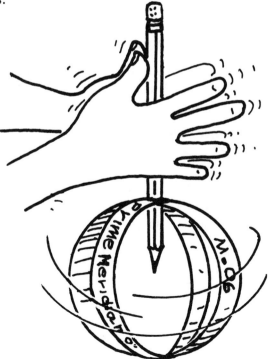

Results Spinning the strips causes the horizontal circumference to increase.

Why? The spinning paper strips undergo a force that causes them to move outward so that they form a shape that is fatter and flatter. Like all rotating spheres, the earth bulges at the center and flattens at the poles. The circumference of the earth at the equator is about 42 miles (67.2 km) greater than the circumference around the North and South Poles.

Solutions to Exercises

1. *Think!*

- Which is the latitude coordinate? Latitudes are measured in degrees north or south. 40°N is the latitude coordinate. Find it on the map.

- Which is the longitude coordinate? Longitudes are measured in degrees west or east. 5°W is the longitude coordinate. Find it on the map.

- Use your finger to trace the latitude 40°N line from the side of the map until it touches the 5°W longitude line. Identify the country where these two lines cross.

40°N, 5°W are coordinates in Spain.

2. *Think!*

- Use your finger to trace the latitude 45°N line from the side of the map until it touches the longitude 25°E line. Identify the country where these two lines cross.

40°N, 25°E are coordinates in Romania.

5

Mapping a Sphere: The Earth

Comparing Globes and Flat Maps

What You Need to Know

The most accurate and realistic map of the earth is a globe. There is less distortion in the distances, directions, and sizes and shapes of the land on a globe than there is on a flat map. But it is difficult to carry around a globe, so cartographers must produce a flat representation of something that is actually curved. They may peel off the outer layer of the globe in one piece and lay it flat. But curved surfaces cannot lie flat unless the globe's surface is cut from top to bottom into equal sections that are long, elliptical, and pointed on each end. Cartographers call these sections **gores**.

The problem lies in transferring details from the separate gores to a single flat map with few errors and distortions. There is going to be some error in every flat map because of the impossibility of making a two-dimensional map that gives an exact picture of a three-dimensional structure. A flat map can be correct in showing either the size of the lands and seas, or their shapes. It cannot show both without some error.

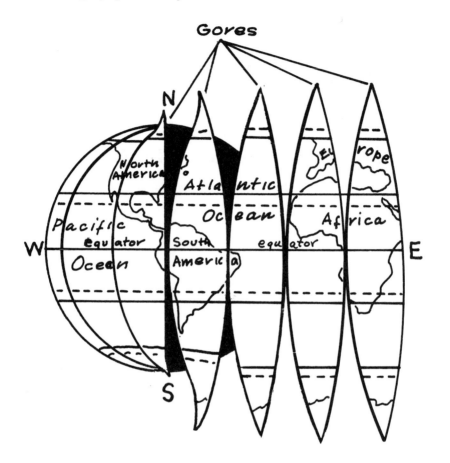

A **map projection** is the means of transferring information about the earth's surface to a flat map. The **Mercator projection map** is best suited to navigation because it gives true directions and accurate shapes of land and water. But it exaggerates the sizes of land that lies at great distances from the equator, such as areas near the North and South poles.

Let's Think It Through

1. Compare the longitude and latitude lines on the globe below with those shown on the Mercator projection map on
the next page.

2. Compare the size of Greenland to South America on the
globe and Mercator projection map.

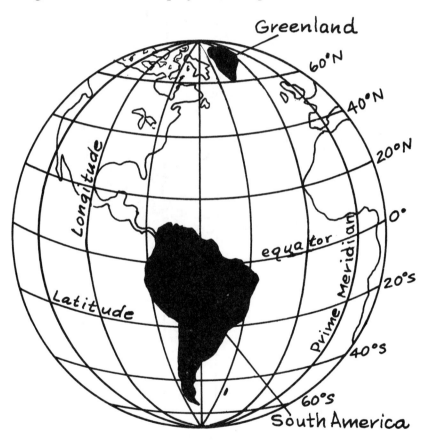

GLOBE

MERCATOR PROJECTION MAP

Answers

Think!

1. The longitude and latitude lines are curved on the globe, but both are straight on the Mercator projection map.

2. The island of Greenland is much smaller than the continent of South America on the globe, but appears to be larger than South America on the Mercator projection map.

Exercises

Draw a Mercator projection map of the landmasses below the equator by using the six-gored map on page 48. Construct your map by following these steps:

1. Trace the grid pattern for the Mercator projection map on page 48 on to a sheet of paper.

2. Draw all landmasses located in each square of the six-gored map onto the same square of the Mercator projection map.

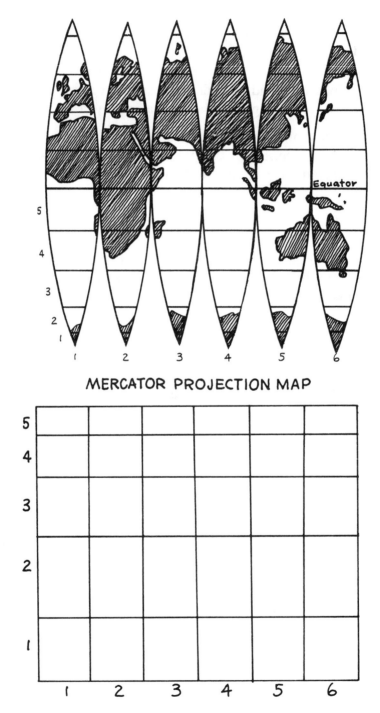

MERCATOR PROJECTION MAP

Activity: SKINNING THE EARTH

Purpose To simulate the cutting of the earth's "skin" into gores to form a flat map.

Materials adult helper
large orange
knife (with an adult's permission)
paper towel
marking pen
tracing paper

Procedure

1. Ask your adult helper to cut the skin of the orange into four equal-sized sections from top to bottom with the knife.

2. Carefully peel off each section in one complete piece and press the outer skin face up on the paper towel.

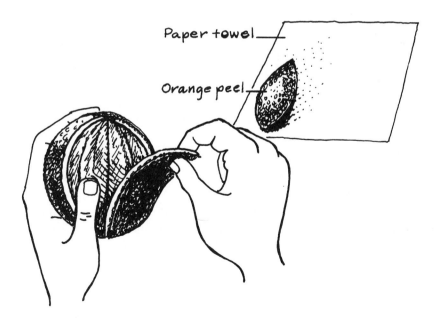

Paper towel

Orange peel

3. Following the four map patterns, draw the land structure of the earth on the four separate pieces of orange peel.

4. Lay the pieces of orange peel side by side and observe how the landmasses fit together.

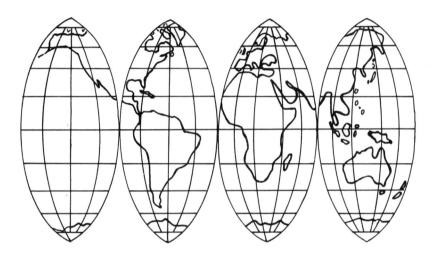

5. Lay a sheet of tracing paper over the orange peel and trace the shape of the land features, extending lines to make boundaries of continents continuous.

Results A flat map of a curved surface is produced.

Why? If you cut the "skin" of the earth into gores and lay them flat, as you did with the orange, you would have the most accurate map of the earth. Tracing the land features on the gores taken from the orange left gaps in what are continuous landmasses. Connecting the boundary lines distorted the actual shape and size of the land features. The amount of distortion is greatest at the poles and least at the equator.

Solutions to Exercises

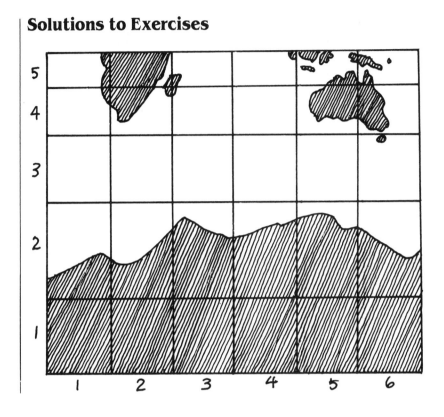

6
Using a Map Scale

Determining the Distance between Two Points on the Earth

What You Need to Know

The illustration shows two maps, one of Africa and the other of Burkina. The map of Africa represents a continent, while the map of Burkina shows one country within a continent. The map of Burkina represents a much smaller area, but looks almost as large as the map of Africa.

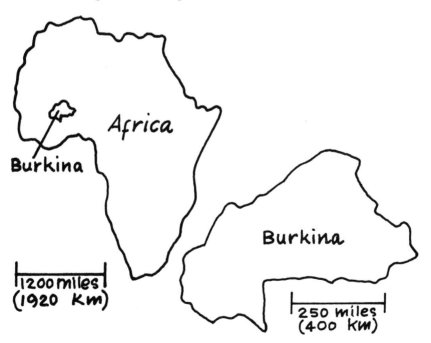

A **scale** is a key on a map that uses a small measure to represent a larger area on the earth. The length of the scale represents a specific distance, usually in miles (kilometers). For example, 1 inch (2.5 cm) on the Burkina map equals 250 miles (400 km) on the earth.

You can use an index card to help you calculate distance on a map. Place the top left corner of the card at the beginning of the scale and mark the point where the scale ends on the card. Mark as many consecutive scale divisions as possible along the edge of the card.

Let's Think It Through

Use the map to determine the distance between Erin's and Tina's houses by measuring between the points marked with an X on the sidewalk.

Mark an index card with the scale from the map. Lay the card along the line that represents the sidewalk between Erin's and

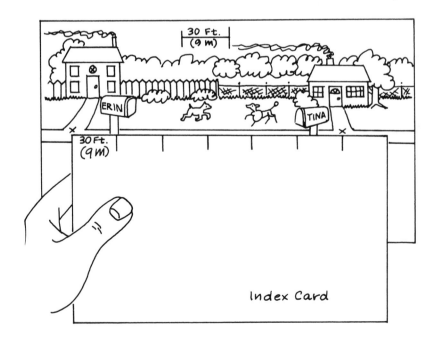

Index Card

Tina's houses. The left edge of the card must be on the X that marks the position of Erin's house. Count the number of marks on the card between the two houses. How far apart in feet (m) are Erin's and Tina's houses?

Answer

Think!

• There are six marks between the houses, and each mark represents 30 feet (9 m).

The distance between the houses is 6 × 30 feet (9 m), or 180 feet (54 m).

Exercises

Use the botanical garden map to determine the distance between the following points:

1. The elm tree and the oak tree.

2. The elm tree and the water lilies (along the paths).

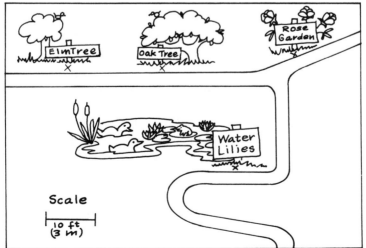

BOTANICAL GARDEN MAP

Activity: FEET

Purpose   To draw a scale model of a room using your feet as the scale.

Materials   your feet
        yardstick (meterstick)
        pencil
        paper

Procedure

1. Place the heel of one foot on top of one end of the stick.

2. Record the length of your foot to the nearest whole inch (cm).

3. Use your feet to measure the width (shorter side) of a room by using the following procedure:

   • Stand with the heel of one foot against one of the longer walls and place the heel of your other foot against your toes. This position is two "feet" from the wall.

   • Lift the back foot and place its heel against the toes of the other foot. This position is three "feet" from the wall.

   • Continue to move in a straight line across the room. Count each step you make by placing one foot directly in front of the other. Count the last step only if it is at least half the length of your foot.

4. Repeat the procedure on an adjacent wall to measure the length (longer side) of the room, the distance perpendicular to the width.

5. Draw a map of the room, using an outline of a foot to represent the map scale, and footprints to indicate the method of measuring the room. Measure the length of your foot to determine the scale at the bottom of the map.

Results   The number of footprints depends on the length and width of the room and how long your feet are. The author's foot is 9 inches (23 cm) long. The room measured by the author is 8 × 11 "feet."

Why?   Most maps contain a scale that looks like a segment of a ruler, but the scale on your map is represented by a foot. The length and width of your room is equal to the number of footprints across multiplied by the length of your foot. The

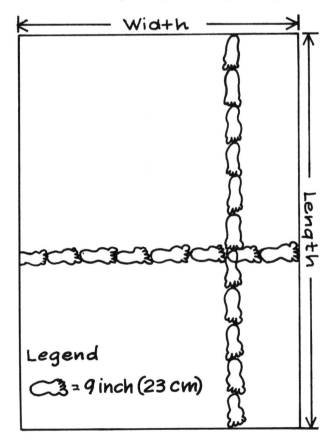

measurements of the author's room would be calculated as follows:

The width is 8 footprints × 9 inches (23 cm), or 72 inches (184 cm).

The length is 11 footprints × 9 inches (23 cm), or 99 inches (253 cm).

Solutions to Exercises

1. *Think!*

- How many scale divisions are there between the elm tree and the oak tree?   Two.

- How far does each scale division represent?   10 feet (3 m).

The distance between the trees is 2 × 10 feet (3 m), or 20 feet (6 m).

BOTANICAL GARDEN MAP

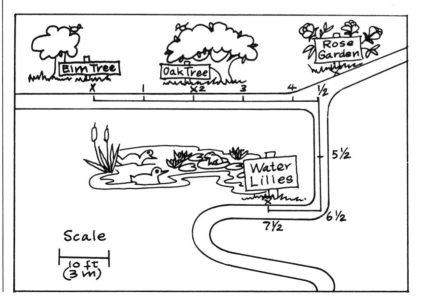

2. *Think!*

• How many scale divisions are there between the elm tree and the water lilies?   7½

• How far does each scale division represent?
10 feet (3 m).

The distance between the elm tree and the water lilies is 7½ × 10 feet (3 m), or ?

• How long is 7 divisions?   7 × 10 feet (3 m), or 70 feet (21 m).

• How long is ½ of a division?   5 feet (1.5 m).

The distance between the elm tree and the water lilies is 70 feet (21 m) + 5 feet (1.5 m), or 75 feet (22.5 m).

7
Finding Places
How to Read and Use a Grid Map

What You Need to Know

Road maps and street maps are often divided into squares of equal size by a grid. These squares are labeled with letters down the side of the map and numbers across the top, as in the map of Fred's Neighborhood.

FRED'S NEIGHBORHOOD

Index

Home	B2
Lake Lauren	A1
Park	A2
School	B1

To read a grid map, find the name of the place you want to visit in the index. The names are listed alphabetically and the name is followed by a letter-number combination that directs you to a specific square on the map. Look inside the square and you will find the name of the place you want to visit.

Let's Think It Through

Use the index to the map of South America to locate the city of Rio de Janeiro.

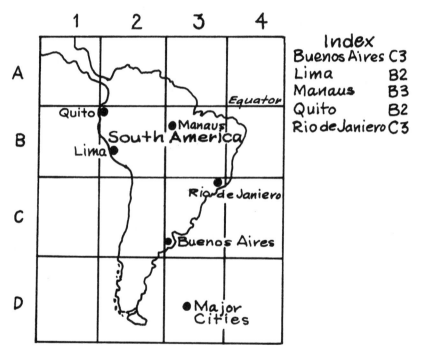

Index
Buenos Aires C3
Lima   B2
Manaus   B3
Quito   B2
Rio de Janiero C3

Answer

Think!

• Find Rio de Janeiro on the Index. It's labeled C3.

• Find the letter C on the left side of the map. All of the blocks in the horizontal row to the right of the letter C are C-squares.

- Find the number 3 at the top of the map. Trace your finger down the squares under the number 3 until it touches the row of C-squares (the third square down from the top).

- Where is Rio de Janeiro within C3?

Rio de Janeiro is in the upper-right corner of C3.

Exercises

1. The legend shows the symbols that represent each building site on the map. Use the legend for the map of Stephenville to find the following places on the map:

   a. The library.

   b. The school.

   c. The science museum.

   What is the index letter-number combination for each?

2. Which is closer to the school, the library or the science museum?

STEPHENVILLE

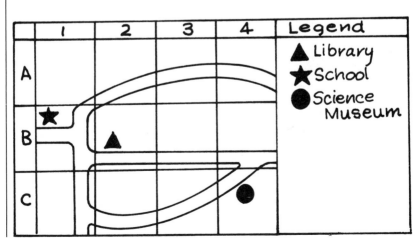

Activity: ENLARGER

Purpose To use a grid to enlarge a picture.

Materials yardstick (meterstick)
marking pen
poster board, 18 inches (45 cm) square
pencil with eraser
crayons
scissors

Procedure

1. Use the measuring stick and pencil to draw a 16-inch (45-cm) line across the top of the paper. The line should be 1 inch (2.5 cm) from the top and 1 inch (2.5 cm) from each side of the paper.

2. Draw four more 16-inch (45-cm) lines parallel with the first line and 4 inches (10 cm) apart.

3. Draw five vertical lines intersecting the horizontal lines, 4 inches (10 cm) apart, to form a grid with 16 squares.

4. Label the squares 1, 2, 3, and 4 across the top, and A, B, C, and D down the side as in the picture of the clown.

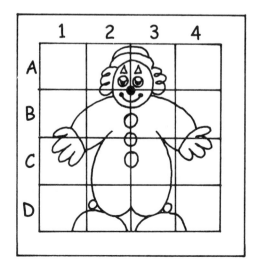

5. To enlarge the picture of the clown, start with square A2 (there are no lines in square A1). Use the pencil to copy the lines in square A2 of the clown picture on square A2 on your paper.

6. Repeat the procedure for square A3.

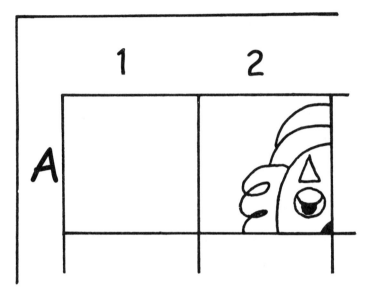

7. Continue until all the lines from the clown picture have been copied.

8. Trace over the pencil lines of the drawing with the marking pen.

9. Erase the grid lines.

10. Color the picture.

11. Cut around the outside of the large square, trimming away the letters and numbers.

Result   An enlarged, colored picture of a clown.

Why? The first picture of the clown has a grid of 16 squares of equal size. The picture you made also has 16 squares, but they are bigger than those in the smaller diagram. Copying the lines in each small block on the corresponding large block allows you to reproduce an accurate enlargement of the original picture.

Solutions to Exercises

1a. *Think!*

- What is the symbol for the library? A triangle.

- In which square is the triangle (library) located?

The library is located in B2.

b. *Think!*

- What is the symbol for the school? A star.

- In which square is the star (school) located?

The school is located in B1.

c. *Think!*

- What is the symbol for the science museum? A circle.

- In which square is the circle (science museum) located?

The science museum is located in C4.

2. The library is closer to the school.

8
Legends

How to Use a Legend When Reading a Map

What You Need to Know

Mapmakers use symbols such as stars to represent state capitals and dots for other cities. Other symbols can stand for camp sites, highways, parks, and so on. Lines, dots, colors, geometric figures, or other designs can represent anything from the number of brown bears to natural or international boundaries. The different symbols are listed in the map's **legend**, a key that works like a decoder to unlock the secret meanings of the map's symbols.

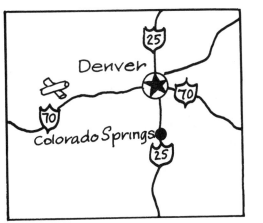

Melville
MANITOBA
Weyburn   Winnepeg ✪
Estevan
CANADA
UNITED STATES
Minot
Williston
NORTH DAKOTA
Bismarck ✪

Legend
— ·· — International Boundary
— · — · — State Boundary
✪ Capitol City
● Principal City

Let's Think It Through

Use the map of North Dakota and Manitoba to answer these questions:

1. What is the capital city of North Dakota?

2. Which two cities are not in the same country?

   a. Estevan and Weyburn

   b. Estevan and Williston

Answers

1. *Think!*

• What is the symbol for capital cities?

A circled star.

• Which city in North Dakota has a circled star by its name?

Bismarck is the capital city of North Dakota.

2. *Think!*

• What is the symbol for the international boundary?

— • • —

• Which answer lists cities on either side of this boundary?

b. Estevan and Williston are not in the same country.

Exercises

Mr. Carney is going on vacation. He has prepared a map of his mail route for Ms. Prior, his substitute. Use his map to answer these questions:

1. On which street will Ms. Prior find no dogs?

2. How many homes have people who sleep during the day?

3. Which streets have unfriendly dogs?

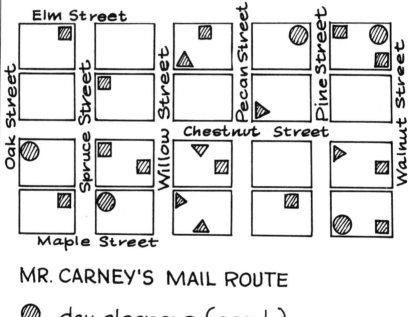

MR. CARNEY'S MAIL ROUTE

◉ day sleepers (people)
▲ unfriendly dog
▨ friendly dog

Activity: PARK MAP

Purpose To prepare a map of a neighborhood park using symbols and a legend.

Materials neighborhood park
ball of string
5 pencils
ruler
sheet of typing paper

Procedure

1. Select an area in the park with as many of these landmarks as possible: trees, bushes, tables, paths, flowers, trash cans, playground equipment, and so on.

2. Use the string and four of the pencils as stakes to mark off a plot about 30 **paces** square. A pace is one giant step.

3. Measure and draw a 6-by-6-inch (15-by-15-cm) box at the top of the sheet of paper.

4. Draw a box below the square with the title "Park Section #1" (you may want to include the name of the park in the title).

5. Under the title, list the landmarks and their symbols. Use the symbols in the diagram, or create your own.

6. Draw the symbol of each landmark in the square approximately where it is located in the plot.

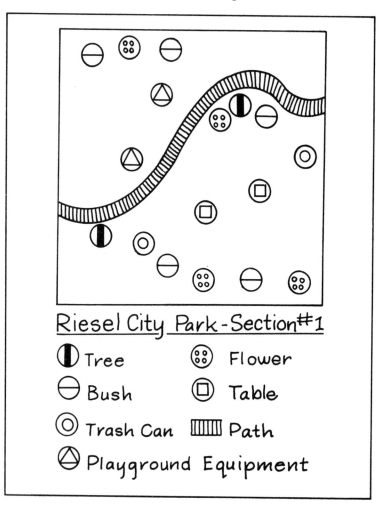

Results   A map with a legend is produced.

Why?   Symbols are used to represent the park's physical features and equipment. The position of each symbol designates the location of each object.

Solutions to Exercises

1. *Think!*

• What are the symbols for dogs?

A square and a triangle.

• Which street does not have a square or triangle symbol?

Ms. Prior will not find any dogs on Oak Street.

2. *Think!*

• What is the symbol for day sleepers?

A circle.

• How many circles are on the map?

Five homes have people who sleep during the day.

3. *Think!*

• What is the symbol for unfriendly dogs?

A triangle.

• Which streets have triangles?

Maple, Willow, Pecan, Pine, and Chestnut streets have unfriendly dogs.

9
Variation

Find the Variation between Geographic North and Magnetic North

What You Need to Know

The **geographic north pole** (the true North Pole) is located at latitude 90°N. It is the point where the earth's imaginary axis breaks through the surface. This axis points toward **Polaris** (the north star). The earth's **magnetic north pole** is located at about 75°N, 101°W. It is the point on the earth's surface toward which the north poles of all magnets are attracted. The angle of difference between the direction toward geographic north and magnetic north from a given point on the earth is called the **angle of magnetic declination** or **variation.** Depending on the location of the observer, the variation can be zero, easterly, or westerly of geographic north. Variation is greater as the observer approaches the poles.

Geographer's Toolbox: VARIATION INDICATOR

Materials   scissors
cardboard
2 straws, one striped, the other colored
pushpin
map showing magnetic north and North poles
adult helper

Construct a variation indicator and use it on a map by following these steps:

Procedure

1. Cut the cardboard into a square slightly wider than one straw.

2. Lay the ends of the straws, one on top of the other, on the cardboard square.

3. Ask your helper to stick a pushpin through both straws and into the cardboard.

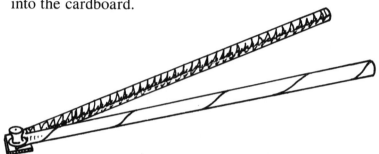

4. Place the cardboard at any point on the map.

5. Pivot the straws so that the colored straw passes over the North Pole and the striped straw passes over the magnetic north pole.

- If the striped straw lies to the right of the colored straw, the variation is easterly.

- If the striped straw lies to the left of the colored straw, the variation is westerly.

- If the straws lie on top of each other, the variation is zero.

Let's Think It Through

Use your variation indicator and the map below to determine the direction of variation from the locations of:

1. Observer A.

2. Observer B.

3. Observer C.

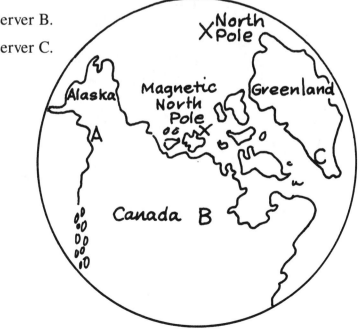

Answers

1. *Think!*

- Is the striped straw to the right or left of the colored straw? It is to the right.

From the location of Observer A, variation is easterly.

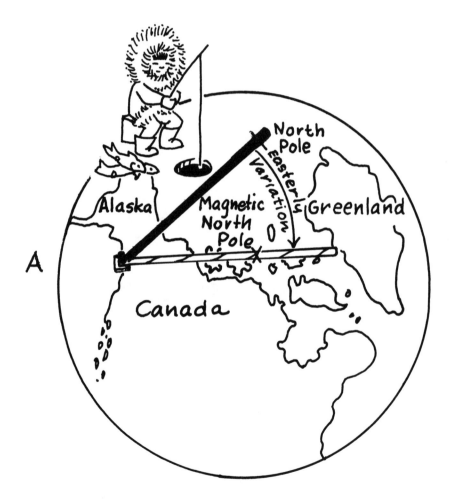

2. *Think!*

• Is the striped straw to the right or left of the colored straw? It is neither to the right or left.

From the location of Observer B, variation is zero.

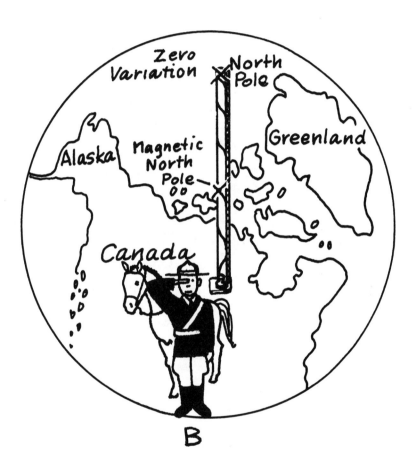

3. *Think!*

* Is the striped straw to the right or left of the colored straw?

  It is to the left.

From the location of Observer C, variation is westerly.

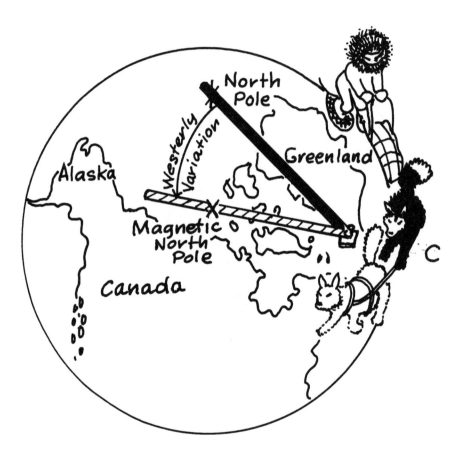

Exercises

Use your variation indicator and the Xs on the map below to determine the direction of variation for the observer at each of these geographic locations:

1. Hawaiian Islands.

2. South America.

3. Africa.

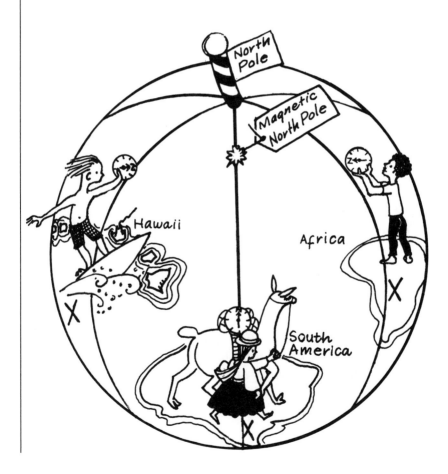

Activity: WHERE IS NORTH?

Purpose To determine the direction of variation for where you live.

Materials scissors
ruler
string
large nail
white poster paper
marking pen
flashlight
compass
helper

Procedure

NOTE: Steps 3–11 of this activity must be performed outdoors on a clear, moonless night.

1. Cut a length of string 12 inches (30 cm) longer than your height.

2. Tie one end of the string to the nail.

3. Lay the paper on the ground.

4. Wrap the free end of the string around the end of your right index finger.

5. Stand on the edge of the paper with your right foot and right index finger pointing toward Polaris. (Find Polaris by following a straight line up from the two outermost stars in the bowl of the Big Dipper. Polaris is directly ahead.)

Polaris

Polaris

6. Ask your helper to draw a straight line from the center of the toe of your right foot to the spot under the hanging nail, holding the flashlight in one hand to illuminate the paper.

7. Mark the spot with an arrowhead and label it "North Pole."

8. Place the compass on the line, turning it until the letter N lines up with the north end of the compass needle.

9. Mark dots on the paper at the north and south ends of the needle.

10. Remove the compass and draw a line between the two dots.

11. Draw an arrowhead at the north end of this line and label it "magnetic north pole."

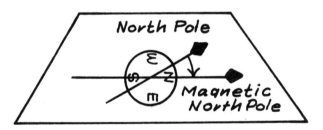

EASTERLY VARIATION FROM TEXAS

Results The direction of variation, which depends on the location of the observer, is determined for where you live. From the author's home in Texas, the variation is easterly.

Why? Polaris is called the north star. This star is directly above the earth's geographic north pole. The north end of the compass needle points toward the earth's magnetic north pole.

The angle between the direction of the lines drawn toward Polaris and the direction of the compass's magnetic needle is the variation for the location where the measurements are taken.

Solutions to Exercises

1. Easterly variation.

2. Zero variation.

3. Westerly variation.

10
Compass Rose

Use a Compass Rose to Measure Direction on a Map

What You Need to Know

A compass rose, used to measure directions, is a circle on which points indicating direction and/or degrees are marked. Each degree mark represents a direction; due north is at 0°, east at 90°, south at 180°, and west at 270°.

Geographer's Toolbox: COMPASS ROSE

Materials tracing paper
marking pen
scissors
sharpened pencil
ruler
string
transparent tape
adult helper

Make a compass rose by following these steps:

Procedure

1. With the tracing paper and pen, carefully trace the diagram of the compass rose on the next page.

2. Cut out the compass rose.

3. Ask your helper to make a small hole in the center of the compass rose with the point of the pencil.

4. Thread an 8-inch (20-cm) piece of string through the hole and tape the end of it to the back of the paper.

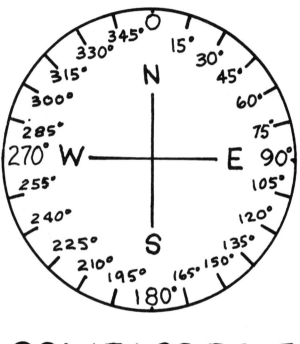

COMPASS ROSE

Let's Think It Through

Use your compass rose and the map of Beaver Park campsites to plot a course from Camp Running Bear to Camp Bluebird.

Answer

Think!

- Place the center of the compass rose over the symbol for Camp Running Bear.

- Turn the compass rose until 0°N is in line with the magnetic north arrow on the map. On most maps, the north arrow points toward the top of the paper.

- Hold the compass rose in place while you pull the string taut and pivot it until it is directly over the symbol for Camp Bluebird.

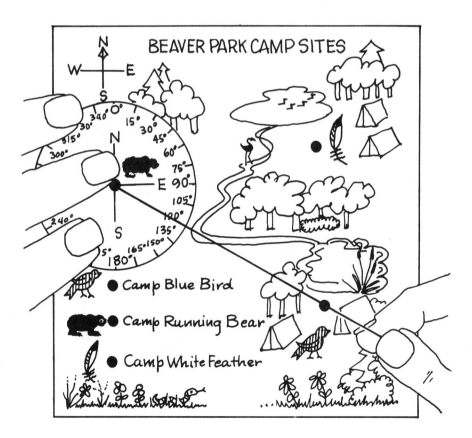

• Read the degree mark that the string passes over on the compass rose.

Camp Bluebird is in a direction 120 degrees away from magnetic north.

Exercises

Use your compass rose and Lacey's map of her neighborhood to plot a course that will take her from:

1. School to her granny's house.

2. Her home to the ice cream shop.

Activity: USING A COMPASS

Purpose   To make a compass with a compass rose and use it to locate magnetic north.

Materials   your compass rose
paper plate
ruler
marking pen
small cereal bowl
tap water
scissors
dishwashing sponge
sewing needle
bar magnet
timer
helper

Procedure

1. Lay the compass rose in the center of the plate.

2. With the ruler and pen, mark 0°, 45°, 90°, 135°, 180°, 225°, 270°, and 315° on the edge of the plate.

3. Label these marks N, NE, E, SE, S, SW, W, and NW.

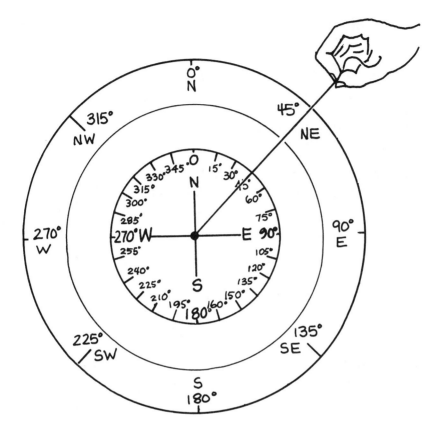

4. Remove the compass rose and lay the plate on a wooden table.

5. Fill the bowl three-fourths full with water.

6. Set the bowl in the center of the paper plate.

7. Cut a 1-by-1-inch (2.5-by-2.5-cm) piece of sponge and place it in the water.

8. Magnetize a sewing needle by laying it on top of a bar magnet for two minutes with the point of the needle at the magnet's north pole.

9. Lay the needle on top of the sponge. Wait one minute.

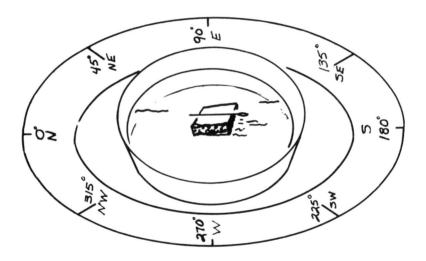

10. Ask your helper to raise the bowl slightly while you rotate the paper plate until the point of the floating needle lines up with the 0° mark on the paper plate.

Results   The tip of the floating magnetic needle points toward 0° (N).

Why?   A **compass** is an instrument used to determine directions by means of a magnetic needle that always points to the earth's magnetic north pole. The main part of a compass is its magnetic needle. The needle must be able to turn freely into a north-south position because the poles of the magnetic needle constantly seek to line up with the earth's magnetic lines of force. The degree marks on the compass rose indicate directions in degrees away from magnetic north. With the compass and compass rose, magnetic north can be located and directions in degrees from one location to another can be determined.

Solutions to Exercises

1. *Think!*

- Place the center of the compass rose over the dot that marks the location of the school.

- Turn the compass rose until 0°N is in line with the magnetic north arrow on the map.

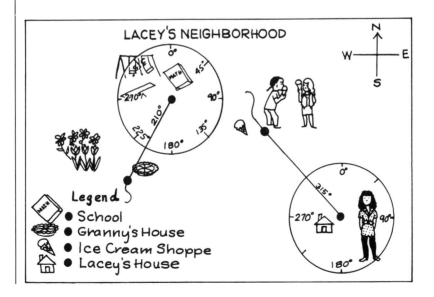

- Pivot the string until it is directly over the dot for granny's house.

- Read the degree mark that the string passes over on the compass rose.

Granny's house is in a direction 210 degrees away from magnetic north.

2. *Think!*

- Follow the steps above to plot a course from Lacey's house to the ice cream shop, starting with the compass rose over the dot that marks the location of Lacey's house and pivoting the string until it is directly over the dot for the ice cream shop.

The ice cream shop is in a direction 315 degrees away from magnetic north.

11
Mapping the Ocean Floor

How to Determine the Depth of the Ocean Floor

What You Need to Know

More than 70 percent of the surface of the earth is covered with water. The earth's ocean floor has mountains, volcanoes, and trenches, as does its land areas. **Ultrasonic waves** (high-frequency sound waves) can be used to reveal the profile of the ocean floor or to find objects such as sunken ships. The

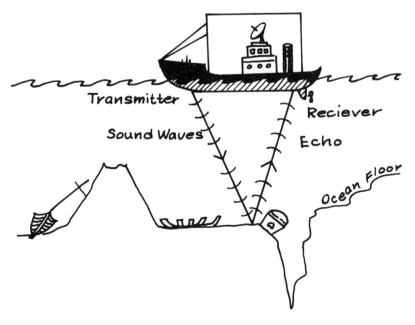

Transmitter

Reciever

Sound Waves

Echo

Ocean Floor

instrument that sends these waves is called a **sonar device**. Sound waves travel in a straight path through water and bounce back when they hit an object. The time it takes them to travel is called the **echo time**, because an echo is heard when they return. Sound waves travel in water at a speed of about 4,800 feet (1.46 km) per second. Since half the trip is a return trip, the distance to the ocean floor can be calculated by multiplying one-half of the speed of sound by the echo time.

Let's Think It Through

In the following questions, calculate the depth of the ocean floor by using this formula:

$$\text{depth} = \tfrac{1}{2} \text{ speed of sound} \times \text{echo time}$$

1. The part of the ocean floor between a continent's shoreline and the ocean's depths is called the **continental shelf**. This area varies in width from almost nothing to about 1,000 miles (1,600 km), averaging about 41 miles (66 km). Calculate the depth of the continental shelf in an area where the echo time is 0.1 second.

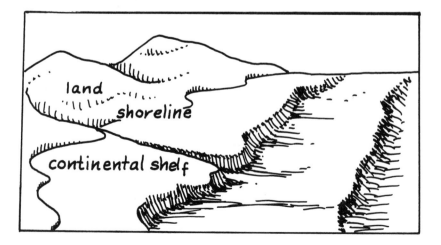

2. The deepest point on the earth lies in the Pacific Ocean south of Guam in a spot in the Mariana Trench called Challenger Deep. Calculate the depth where the echo time is 15 seconds.

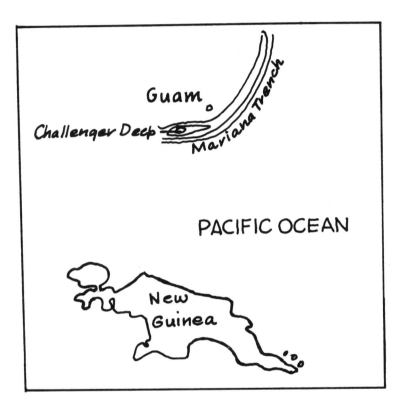

Answers

1. *Think!*

- **English**

  depth in feet = ½ × 4,800 × 0.1
  ½ × 4,800 = 2,400
  2,400 × 0.1 = ?

  depth in feet = 240 feet

- **Metric**

    depth in km = ½ × 1.46 × 0.1
    ½ × 1.46   = 0.73
    0.73 × 0.1 = ?

    depth in km   = 0.073 km

2. *Think!*

- **English**

    depth in feet = ½ × 4,800 × 15
    ½ × 4,800 = 2,400
    2,400 × 15 = ?

    depth in feet = 36,000 feet

- **Metric**

    depth in km = ½ × 1.46 × 15
    ½ × 1.46   = 0.73
    0.73 × 15 = ?

    depth in km   = 10.95 km

Exercises

Use the depth formula to calculate the ocean depth in each of the following questions:

depth = ½ speed of sound × echo time

1. Sound waves were emitted from the sonar device on board a ship. Calculate the depth of the ocean where the echo time is 4 seconds.

2. The continental shelf is a region of great economic importance. Not only does it supply most of the world's seafood, but in many areas it also contains valuable oil deposits. Offshore oil drilling is common along the Pacific

and Gulf coast lines of the United States. Determine the water depth for an offshore oil rig if the echo time is 0.2 seconds.

Activity: HOW DEEP?

Purpose To map the surface of a simulated ocean floor.

Materials scissors
ruler
white string
washer
black marking pen
2-quart (2-liter) glass baking dish, 3 inches (7.6 cm) deep
2 or 3 rocks (must fit inside the baking dish)
pitcher of tap water
pencil
ruled paper
graph paper

Procedure

1. Cut a 12-inch (30-cm) piece of string.

2. Tie one end of the string to a washer.

3. Use the pen and ruler to mark off a ½-inch (1-cm) scale along the string.

4. Set the baking dish on a table, and place the rocks in it.

5. Fill the dish with water. This represents the ocean.

6. Lay the ruler lengthwise on the dish. The edge of the dish represents the shore.

7. Holding the free end of the string, position it against the ruler and next to the edge of the dish (this is the 0-inch mark) and slowly lower the string into the water until the washer touches a rock or the bottom of the bowl.

8. Use the scale marked on the string to determine the depth of the water. Round off the measurement to the nearest scale marking.

9. Measure the depth of the water every ½-inch (1.25 cm) across the length of the dish, and record the measurements in a chart like the one shown.

DATA CHART

Distance from the Shore	Depth
0.0 inch (0.0 cm)	3 inches (7.5 cm)
0.5 inches (1.25 cm)	3 inches (7.5 cm)
1.0 inches (2.5 cm)	2 inches (5.0 cm)

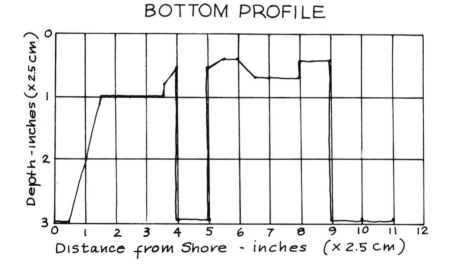

BOTTOM PROFILE

10. Use your data chart to make a graph of your measurements like the one shown.

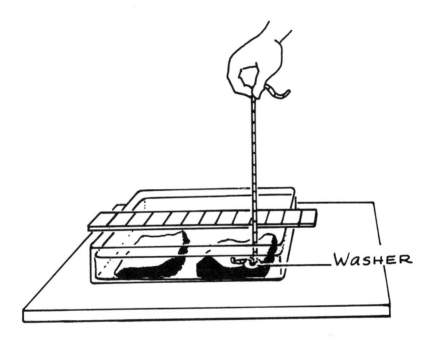

WasHER

Results A graph showing the jagged profile of the dish "floor" is produced.

Why? Dropping the string in the water simulates taking sonar readings at different horizontal distances from the ocean shoreline. The profile made from these readings is jagged because the depth is measured only at intervals instead of along a continuous line. The more measurements taken, the more accurate the profile.

Methods other than sonar are used to study the ocean floor. Underwater laboratories enable scientists to study the ocean floor at close range, but photos taken from satellites in space provide the most accurate picture. Different colors on the photos indicate varying depths.

Solutions to Exercises

1. *Think!*

- **English**

  depth in feet= ½ × 4,800 × 4
  ½ × 4,800= 2,400
  2,400 × 4= ?

  depth in feet= 9,600 feet

- **Metric**

  depth in km= ½ × 1.46 × 4
  ½ × 1.46= 0.73
  0.73 × 4 = ?

  depth in km= 2.92 km

2. *Think!*

- **English**

  depth in feet= ½ × 4,800 × 0.2
  ½ × 4,800= 2,400
  2,400 × 0.2= ?

  depth in feet= 480 feet

- **Metric**

  depth in km= ½ × 1.46 × 0.2
  ½ × 1.46= 0.73
  0.73 × 0.2= ?

  depth in km= 0.146 km

12
Contour Mapping
How to Determine Elevation on a Topographic Map

What You Need to Know

A **topographic map** indicates the shape and elevation of features of the earth's surface, such as mountains, lakes, rivers, roads, and cities. **Contour lines** on a topographic map are irregular loops that connect points of equal elevation. **Elevation** is the **altitude** (height) or depth of the land above a reference point, usually sea level. The **contour interval** (change between the lines) represents **grade** (steepness). The closer the lines, the steeper the grade.

A topographic map can combine colors, patterns, and contour lines to indicate location, shape, and elevation. The profile map of Mount Bald Eagle uses patterns to indicate elevation intervals of 2,000 feet (0.61 km). The contour map is a bird's-eye view of the same mountain.

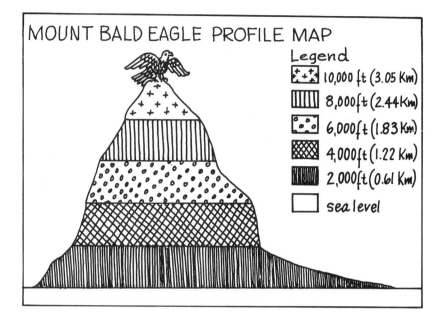

MOUNT BALD EAGLE PROFILE MAP

Legend
- 10,000 ft (3.05 Km)
- 8,000 ft (2.44 Km)
- 6,000 ft (1.83 Km)
- 4,000 ft (1.22 Km)
- 2,000 ft (0.61 Km)
- sea level

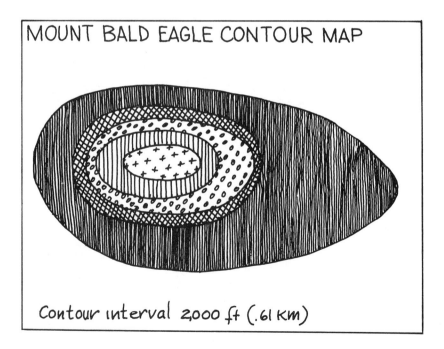

MOUNT BALD EAGLE CONTOUR MAP

Contour interval 2,000 ft (.61 Km)

Let's Think It Through

The profile map of Sea Breeze Island shows one side of the underwater base of the island.

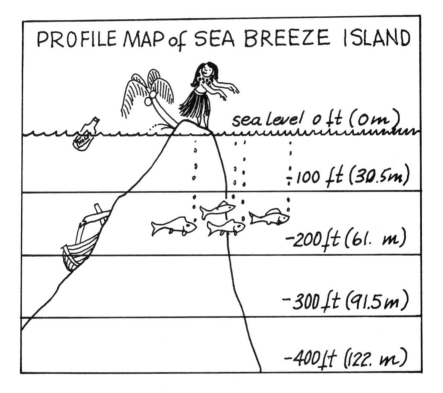

PROFILE MAP of SEA BREEZE ISLAND

sea level 0 ft (0m)

÷100 ft (30.5m)

−200 ft (61. m)

−300 ft (91.5m)

−400 ft (122. m)

Use the marine contour map of Sea Breeze Island on the next page to answer the following questions:

1. Do all the sides of the undersea mountain that forms Sea Breeze Island have steep grades?

2. On which side does the undersea mountain have the most gentle grade?

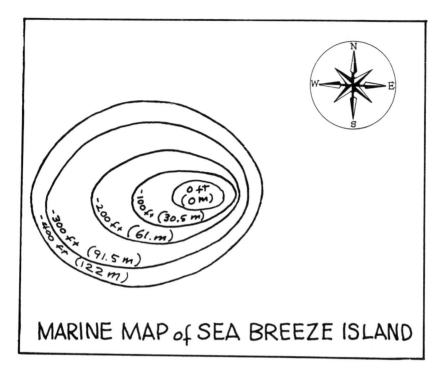

MARINE MAP of SEA BREEZE ISLAND

Answers

1. *Think!*

- Close contour lines indicate a steep grade. Are all the contour lines close together? No. Only one side of the map shows close contour lines.

Only one side of the undersea mountain has a steep grade.

2. *Think!*

- The farther apart the contour lines, the gentler the grade. Which side has the greater distance between the contour lines?

The west side has a gentle grade.

Exercises

The contour interval for each of the three land features mapped in the illustration is 100 feet (30.5 m). Use the maps to answer the following questions:

1. Which feature is more representative of a **mesa** (a hill with a flat top and at least one side that is a steep cliff)?

2. Which feature is tallest?

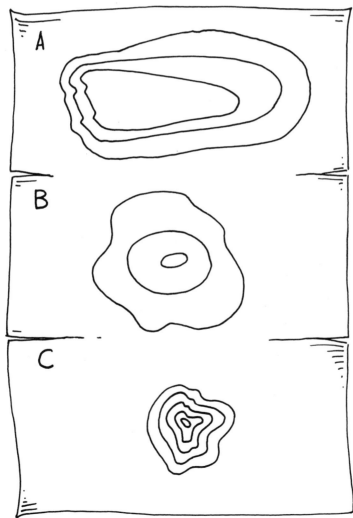

Activity: BELOW THE SURFACE

Purpose To construct a contour map of undersea mountains.

Materials modeling clay
2-quart (2-liter) glass baking dish, 3 inches (7.6 cm) deep
masking tape
marking pen
2-quart (2-liter) pitcher
tap water
spoon
blue food coloring
clear plastic report folder

Procedure

1. Use the modeling clay to mold the shape of two mountains in the bottom of the baking dish. They must not be taller than the dish.

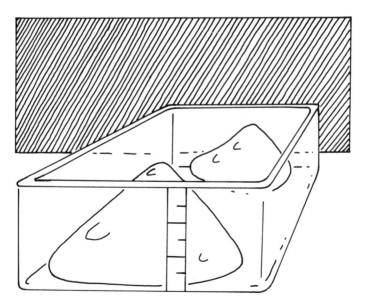

2. Place a strip of masking tape down one side of the dish.

3. Mark off a ½-inch (1.3-cm) scale on the tape from the bottom up.

4. Fill the pitcher with tap water and stir in drops of food coloring until the water is dark blue.

5. Lay the folder over the top of the dish.

6. Standing so that you are looking straight down into the dish, draw the outline of the top of the dish on the folder.

7. Remove the folder and add the colored water up to the first ½-inch (1.3-cm) mark.

8. Put the folder back over the dish and draw the outline of the water line around the clay on the folder.

9. Remove the folder and add more colored water up to the next ½-inch (1.3-cm) mark.

10. Again, draw the outline of the water on the folder.

11. Continue this procedure until the water reaches the top measurement on the tape.

Results The tracing you have made is a topographic map of the mountains in the dish.

Why? Each line on the folder is a contour line connecting points of equal depth on the clay mountains. The contour interval, or the altitude change between the contour lines, is ½ inch (1.3 cm).

Solutions to Exercises

1. *Think!*

- What characterizes a mesa? A flat top and at least one steep side.

- How is a flat top indicated on a contour map? By a large, center contour circle.

- How is steepness indicated? Close contour lines.

- Which map best describes a flat top with at least one steep side?

Map A's land feature is most representative of a mesa.

2. *Think!*

- How is the difference in elevation indicated on a contour map? By the number of contour lines.

- Which map has the most contour lines, and thus represents the tallest feature?

Map C's land feature is tallest.

13
Hurricane Tracking

Tracking the Path of a Hurricane to Predict Where It Will Hit Land

What You Need to Know

A **hurricane** is a tropical **cyclone** (a strong wind blowing in a circle) with winds of 74 miles per hour (118 kmph) or more. It is one of the earth's most awesome storms and the only one given a personal name. A hurricane's development can take about one week, beginning in the tropics as several thunderstorms. When the winds start to spin the clouds in a circle at a speed of less than 39 miles per hour (62 kmph), the storm is considered a **tropical depression**. When the winds reach a speed of 39 miles per hour (62 kmph), the storm is called a **tropical storm** and officially named. When the winds reach a speed of 74 miles per hour (118 kmph), it is classified as a hurricane. On average, 100 tropical storms develop in the world

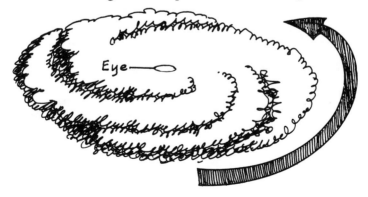

each year, two-thirds grow into tropical cyclones. When fully formed, a hurricane is usually 200–300 miles (320–480 km) across. In the center of the swirling wind is a calm area of clear skies called the **eye of the storm**.

On the average, tropical cyclones in the Northern Hemisphere move from east to west and then head northeast. This turning point gives **meteorologists** (scientists who study weather patterns) clues about if and where the storm will hit land. These predictions have helped reduce the number of hurricane

MAP OF

deaths in the United States, but the cost of hurricanes has risen due to an increase in population along coastal areas.

A hurricane is also called a typhoon, or cyclone, depending on its origin. Typhoons originate in the Pacific, cyclones in the Indian Ocean, and hurricanes in the Atlantic Ocean. On average more than half of the world's tropical cyclones each year form in the Pacific Ocean with about 12 percent in the Atlantic Ocean and 24 percent in the Indian Ocean.

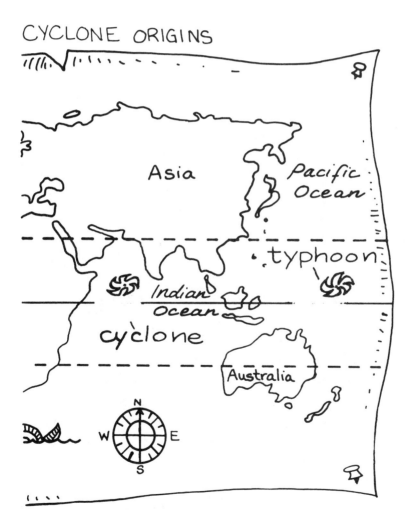

CYCLONE ORIGINS

Let's Think It Through

Use the Hurricane Tracking Map 1 to answer the following questions:

1. What are the coordinates (in latitude and longitude) of the storm at each plotted date?

2. Use the portion of the map on this page to predict which city is in the projected path of the storm on August 12.

Answers

1. *Think!*

- What degrees of latitude and longitude intersect at the five points?

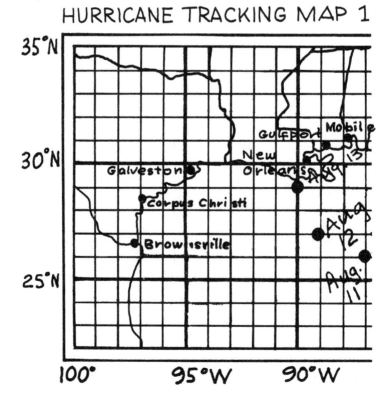

HURRICANE TRACKING MAP 1

Date	Position
August 9	24°N, 83°W
August 10	25°N, 85°W
August 11	26°N, 87°W
August 12	27°N, 89°W
August 13	29°N, 90°W

2. *Think!*

- If a straight line is drawn between the plotted points for August 11 and 12 (be sure *not* to include August 13) and extended forward, which coastal city is on or closest to the line?

Galveston, Texas, is in the projected path of the storm.

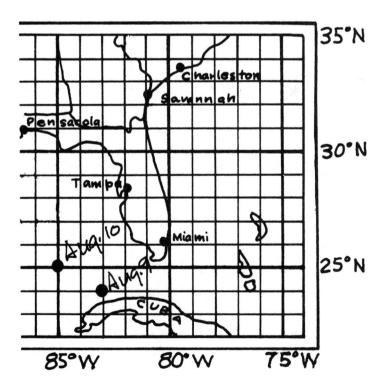

Exercises

1. Lay a sheet of tracing paper over Hurricane Tracking Map 2 and plot the location of Hurricane Kate for each date.

Date	Position	Wind Speed
September 2	23°N, 62°W	50 miles per hour (80 kmph)
September 3	24°N, 64°W	65 miles per hour (104 kmph)

HURRICANE TRACKING MAP 2

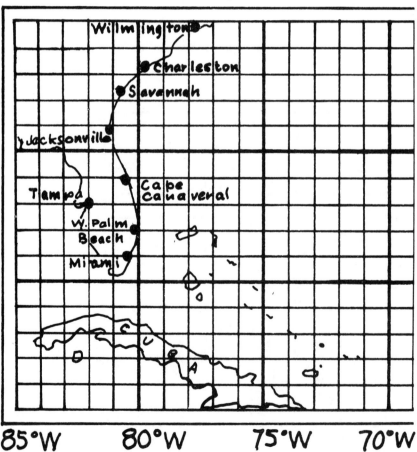

September 4   25°N, 66°W   76 miles per hour (122 kmph)

September 5   26°N, 68°W   90 miles per hour (144 kmph)

2. Move the tracing of the map to the left so that the edges of the maps line up. Which city is closest to the projected path of the storm on September 5?

3. On which date did "Kate" become a hurricane?

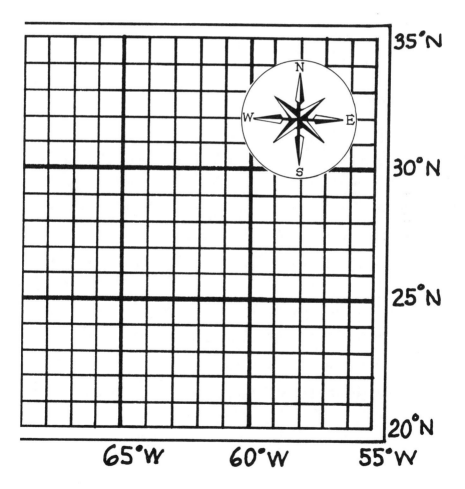

Activity: EYE OF THE STORM

Purpose To demonstrate the calmness in the eye of a hurricane.

Materials scissors
ruler
12-inch (30-cm) piece of sewing thread
paper clip
washer with the same circumference as the
mouth of the bottles
two 2-liter soda bottles
duct tape
tap water
spoon
helper

Procedure

1. Cut a 12-inch (30-cm) piece of thread.

2. Tie the thread to the end of the paper clip. Set the threaded clip aside until you reach step 10.

3. Place the washer over the mouth of one of the bottles.

4. Cut off the bottom of the second bottle.

5. Place the second bottle upside-down on top of the first bottle.

6. Secure the bottles together with tape.

7. Stand the bottles in a sink with the open end up.

8. Fill the top bottle with water.

9. Ask your helper to stir the water with the spoon in a circular direction a few times.

10. While the water is swirling, quickly suspend the paper clip in the center of the swirling water, making every effort not to allow the clip to touch the water.

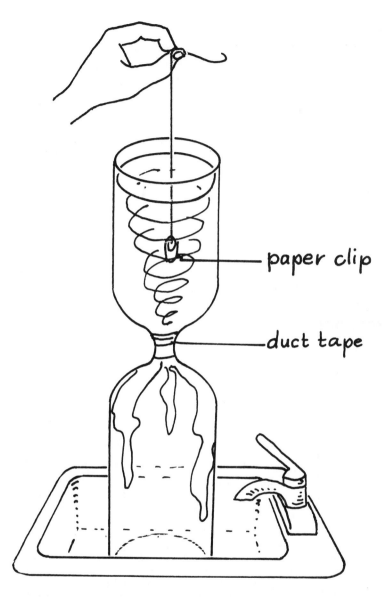

paper clip

duct tape

HOMEMADE HURRICANE

Results   The calmness at the eye of a hurricane is demonstrated. As long as it remains suspended in the funnel of air surrounded by the swirling water, the paper clip is unaffected by the water's movement. If it touches the water, the clip swirls with it.

Why?   The funnel of air in the center of the swirling water, like the funnel-shaped hole in the center of water running down a drain, simulates the eye of a hurricane. The eye of a hurricane is about 20 miles (32 km) across in the middle of the storm, with few if any clouds. It is a long tube of calm all the way to the surface of the earth, with high-speed winds spinning around it. Like the air in a hurricane's eye, the air in the center of the swirling water in the bottle is calm, as indicated by the paper clip's lack of movement.

Solutions to Exercises

1.   HURRICANE TRACKING MAP 2

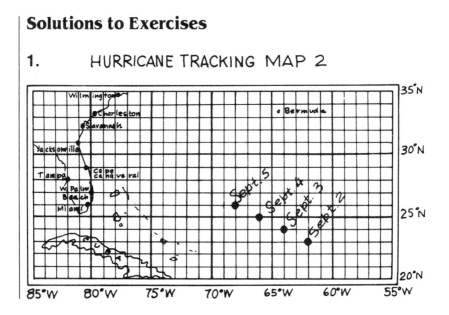

2. *Think!*

- If a straight line is drawn between the plotted points and extended forward, which coastal city is on or closest to the line?

Savannah is closest to the projected path of the storm.

3. *Think!*

- At what speed does a tropical storm become a hurricane? 74 miles per hour (118 kmph).

- When did the storm reach hurricane speed?

Kate became a hurricane on September 4.

14
Seasons

How the Sun Affects the Seasons

What You Need to Know

The earth is in constant motion. One of the many different ways the earth moves is **rotation**, which means that the earth spins around like a top on an imaginary axis running through the earth from the North Pole to the South Pole. The earth makes one rotation every 24 hours, causing day and night. The half of the earth facing the sun receives light, but the opposite side is in the dark.

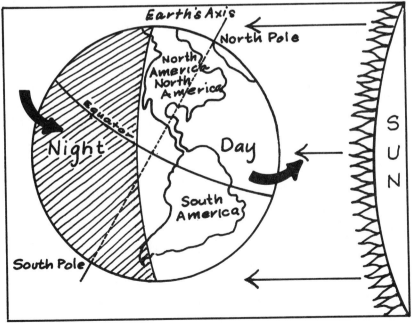

Another way the earth (and any celestial body) moves is **revolution**, which means that it moves around another object. The earth makes one revolution every 365 days, or once a year, around the sun. Because the earth's axis is tilted, direct rays from the sun hit different parts of the earth at different times of the year. When the **Northern Hemisphere** (region north of the equator) leans toward the sun, the **Southern Hemisphere** (region south of the equator) leans away from the sun.

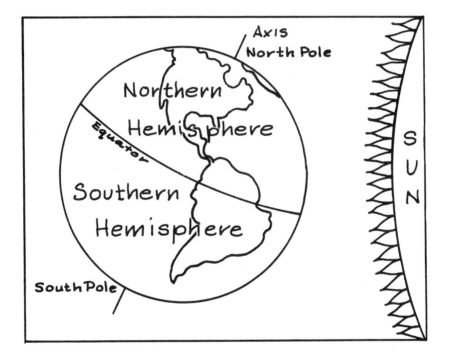

As the tilted earth revolves around the sun, the sun's direct rays strike different parts of the earth, causing the change of seasons (spring, summer, fall, and winter). On June 22, the first day of summer in the Northern Hemisphere, the **Tropic of Cancer** (latitude 23½ degrees north) is the point farthest north of the equator to receive direct solar rays. The point at which the sun is fartherest north from the equator is called the **summer solstice**.

June 22

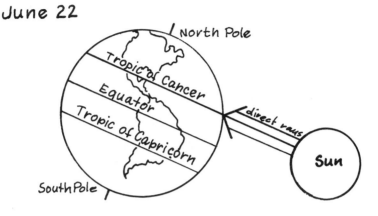

On December 22, the first day of winter in the Northern Hemisphere, the rays center directly on the **Tropic of Capricorn** (latitude 23½ degrees south). On this day the sun is in its **winter solstice** position.

December 22

The **vernal equinox** and **autumnal equinox** are the points through which the sun passes during its apparent path on the first day of spring (March 21) and autumn (September 23), respectively, in the Northern Hemisphere. The sun's rays center directly on the equator on these two dates (as shown on page 128), and day and night are of equal length.

March 21

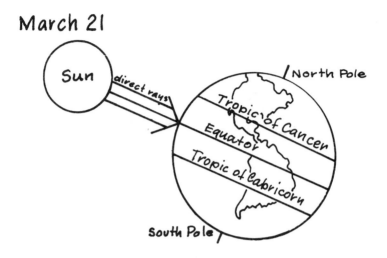

September 23

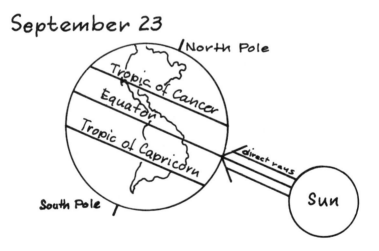

Let's Think It Through

Use the diagram to answer the following questions:

1. In position C, which hemisphere, northern or southern, is in winter?

2. In which position is it winter in the Southern Hemisphere?

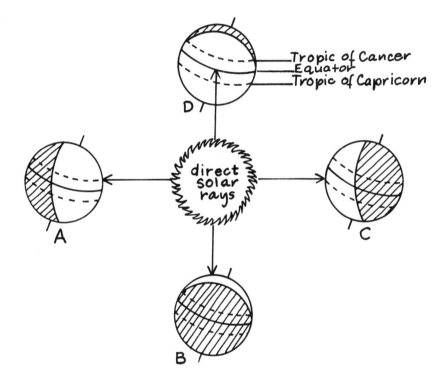

Answers

1. *Think!*

- The hemisphere that leans away from the sun's direct rays is in its winter season. Which hemisphere is leaning away from the sun's rays in position C?

The Northern Hemisphere is in winter.

2. *Think!*

- In which position is the Southern Hemisphere leaning away from the sun?

It is winter in the Southern Hemisphere in position A.

Exercises

Based on the position of the earth in the diagram below, pick the appropriate seasonal scene shown at right to answer the following questions:

1. Which scene best represents the season in New York?

2. Which scene best represents the season in Buenos Aires?

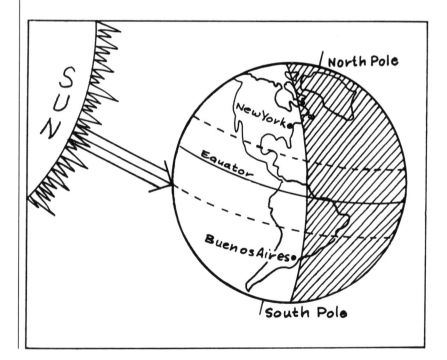

Activity: SUN SPOTS

Purpose To determine why the earth is cooler in winter.

Materials flashlight
1 sheet of dark-colored paper
chalk
helper

Procedure

1. In a dark room, hold the flashlight about 6 inches (15 cm) directly above the paper.

2. Ask you helper to draw a chalk line around the lighted area of the paper.

SUMMER RAYS

3. Label this line "summer rays."

4. Keep the flashlight at the same distance from the paper but tilt it slightly.

5. Again ask your helper to draw a line around the lighted area.

6. Label this line "winter rays."

WINTER RAYS

summer rays

Results   A small, bright circle of light is produced when the flashlight is held straight above the paper. Tilting the flashlight produces a larger, less bright area of light on the paper.

Why?   The sun, as represented by the flashlight, produces more light and thus more warmth when it is directly overhead as it is in the summer. In winter, the position of the sun in the sky is not as high as it is in summer. Winter sunlight comes in at an angle, like the light from the slanted flashlight. This light travels through more of the atmosphere and covers a larger area of the earth than the direct summer rays. Because more of the atmosphere is heated before reaching the earth's surface and a larger area of the surface is heated, the area hit by slanted rays does not get as hot as when direct sun rays strike it.

In the summer, our region of the earth (Northern Hemisphere) leans toward the sun. Because of this tilt, the region receives more direct sun rays, and thus more heat and light. In the winter, our region leans away from the sun, and thus receives fewer direct rays.

Solutions to Exercises

1. *Think!*

- New York is in the Northern Hemisphere, which is tilted away from the sun's rays.

- Thus, it is winter in New York.

Scene D best represents the season in New York.

2. *Think!*

- Buenos Aires is in the Southern Hemisphere, which is tilted toward the sun's rays.

- Thus, it is summer in Buenos Aires.

Scene B best represents the season in Buenos Aires.

15
Time Zones
Compare the Differences in Time for a Traveler Going East or West

What You Need to Know

Since earliest recorded history, people have used the movements of celestial bodies as points of reference when measuring time. The apparent movement of the sun, and changes in

SUNDIAL

the shape of the moon and position of stars have all been used to measure time. The sun seems to be the easiest to follow, because the earth's rotation during the day makes it appear that the sun is moving across the sky. Thus, instruments such as the sundial can be used to determine the position of the sun and indicate time.

For thousands of years, noon has been considered the time when the sun reaches its highest position in the sky. Because the earth is a rotating sphere, the sun cannot be directly over London and New York at the same time. Noon comes first in the eastern city of London because the earth rotates toward the east.

As people began to venture farther from their homes, they noticed that "local time" varied from city to city. In the later 1800s, across the United States there were more than 50 different local times. Since it takes 24 hours for the earth to make one rotation, Stanford Fleming, a Canadian, suggested

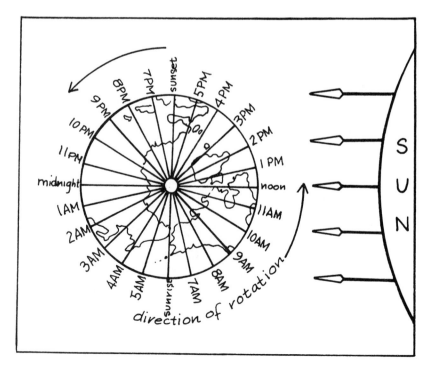

dividing the earth into 24 time zones. In 1884, a group of countries established standard time zones for the whole earth. Each zone is about 15 degrees of longitude wide, with adjustments made in some locations so that a city or small country is not divided into two zones. Clocks to the east of a time zone are set for one hour later; clocks to the west, one hour earlier.

If you could stop time for a moment and see what people are doing all over the world, you would find people in New York having lunch on Monday while people in London are preparing for dinner. Continuing east around the globe, families in Tokyo, Japan, are sleeping in the wee hours of Tuesday morning. In Velen, Siberia, at 6 A.M. on Tuesday families are sitting down to breakfast. Only a few miles away, families in Nome, Alaska, are also having breakfast, but it is Monday morning. It is the same time in both locations, but because the two cities are on opposite sides of the **international date line** (an imaginary line located at longitude 180°), it is always one day later to the west of this line.

INTERNATIONAL DATE LINE

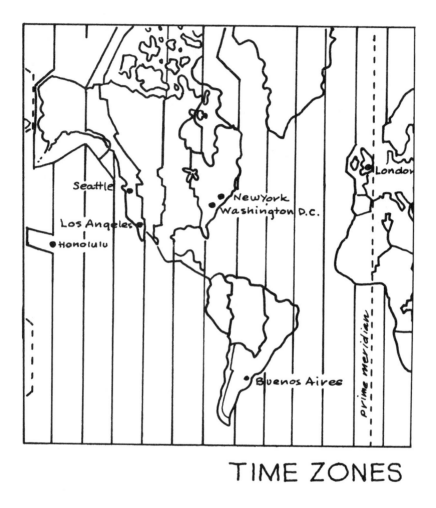

TIME ZONES

Let's Think It Through

Use the map above to answer the following questions:

1. When it is noon in London, what time is it in New York City?

2. It is 7:00 A.M. in Sydney and Brisbane. If it is Wednesday in Sydney, what day is it in Brisbane?

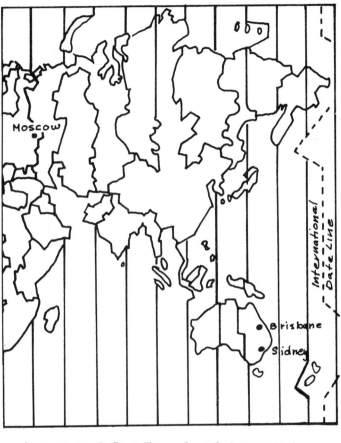

ACROSS THE EARTH

Answers

1. *Think!*

- Locate London and New York on the map.

- How many time zones are there between these two cities? Six.

- Is New York to the west or east of London? New York is to the west of London, thus it is at an earlier time.

It is 7:00 A.M. in New York.

2. *Think!*

- Locate Brisbane and Sydney on the map. How many time zones are there between these two cities? They are in the same zone.

- Does the international date line separate the cities? No.

The day in both cities is Wednesday.

Exercises

Use the United States Time Zones map to determine the time in the following cities when it is 3:00 P.M. in Houston:

1. San Francisco.

2. Atlanta.

Activity: TIME

Purpose   To study the relationship between the apparent motion of the sun and time.

Materials   scissors
ruler
butcher paper
basketball
marking pen
transparent tape
straw
modeling clay
flashlight

Procedure

1. Cut a strip of paper 4 inches (10 cm) wide and long enough to wrap around the basketball.

2. Fold the strip into 3 equal sections.

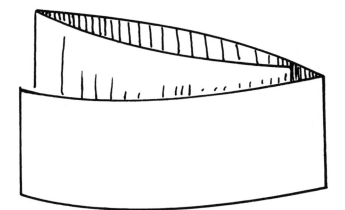

3. Fold it in half to form 6 equal sections.

4. Fold it in half two more times to form 24 equal sections.

5. Unfold the strip and draw a line on each crease.

6. Wrap the strip around the basketball and secure the ends together with a piece of tape.

7. Cut three 2-inch (5-cm) pieces from the straw.

8. Use three dabs of clay to stand the straw pieces on three consecutive sections of the strip.

9. Turn on the flashlight and lay it on the edge of a table with the bulb facing outward.

10. Darken the room.

11. Standing with the flashlight to your right, hold the basketball so that it is about 6 inches (15 cm) away from the bulb and the first straw points straight toward you.

12. Observe the shadows of the straws on the paper.

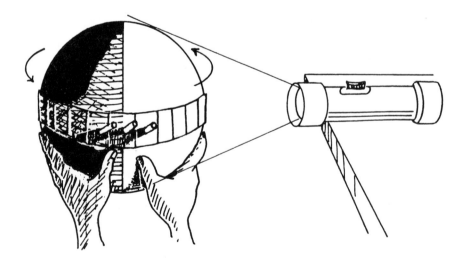

13. Continue to observe their shadows as you slowly rotate the ball to the right. Stop when the first straw points directly at the light.

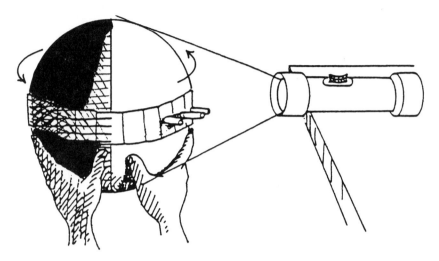

Results   Shadows are cast by the straws. Straws closer to the light have shorter shadows.

Why?   As the straws get closer to the light, their shadows shorten until no shadow is cast by the straw pointing directly at the light. This is a simulation of the earth rotating on its axis toward the sun with each of the 24 sections on the paper representing one time zone. The difference in the shadows indicates a difference in distance from the noonday sun when the sun is directly overhead, and thus a difference in time.

Solutions to Exercises

1. *Think!*

- Locate Houston and San Francisco on the map. How many time zones are there between these two cities? Two. A separation of two time zones indicates a difference of two hours between the two cities.

- Is San Francisco to the west or east of Houston? It is to the west of Houston. Thus, it is at an earlier time.

The time in San Francisco is 1:00 P.M.

2. *Think!*

- Locate Houston and Atlanta on the map. How many time zones are there between these two cities? One. A separation of one time zone indicates a difference of one hour between the two cities.

- Is Atlanta to the west or east of Houston? Atlanta is to the east of Houston. Thus, it is at a later time.

The time in Atlanta is 4:00 P.M.

16
Atmospheric Circulation

Determine How the Circulation of the Earth's Atmosphere Affects Climate

What You Need to Know

The earth's atmosphere is a blanket of **air** (a mixture of gases) surrounding the earth. Because of the uneven heating of the earth's surface by the sun (see Chapter 14 for more information about this), the **climate** (the pattern of weather that one region has over a long period of time) is hot year-round at the equator, cold year-round in the polar regions, and milder between these two regions. The temperature of the atmosphere surrounding the earth is likewise warmest above the equator and coldest at the poles. A basic scientific rule regarding air is that warm air rises and cold air sinks. The hot air at the equator rises. As it moves into a higher altitude, it cools and sinks back to the earth. When the hot air rises, the sinking colder air rushes in to take its place. The movement of the air is called **wind**. Winds are a very important factor in climate. In the Northern Hemisphere, southern winds bring northward the warmth from Mexico and the Caribbean, while northern winds bring southward the bitter cold of the arctic region. Winds transport the temperature of one place to another, making it warmer or colder than it would otherwise be.

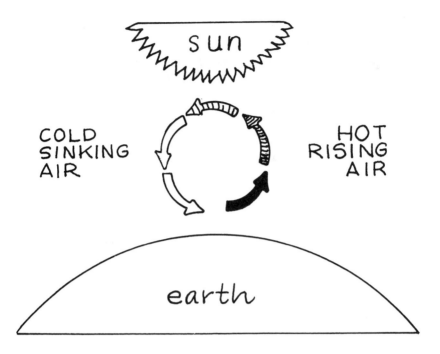

The movement of air around the earth creates a global energy balance. Without air movement, the equatorial region would continue to get hotter while the polar regions got colder. The earth's organisms could not live in these extreme temperatures. The climates around the earth vary little from year to year because the hot air from the equator continues to flow toward the poles while the colder air from the poles moves toward the equator.

The wind patterns between the equator and the polar regions would only be in a north or south direction were it not for the rotation of the earth. The earth's rotation causes the winds to deflect, or bend, producing what is called the **Coriolis effect**. Surface winds are deflected to the right in the Northern Hemisphere and to the left in the Southern Hemisphere. Imagine yourself standing at 30°N on the wind pattern diagram. If you look toward the North Pole, your right hand would be pointing east, just as winds blowing north from the 30°N latitude are deflected to the east. If you turn around and face the equator, your right hand would be pointing west, just as winds blowing south from the 30°N latitude are deflected to the west. You can use this same mental exercise of facing in the direction of the wind to reason out the east and west deflection of the other wind patterns shown in the diagram.

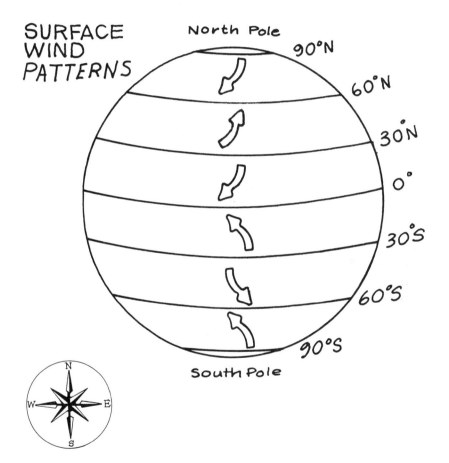

Let's Think It Through

Because there is little surface wind near the equator as the hot air rises, this area is called the **doldrums** (listless). Early sailors feared crossing into the doldrums and possibly being stranded there for long time periods.

Trace the diagram of the Northern Hemisphere and use arrows to show the cyclic winds between the doldrums and latitude 30°N.

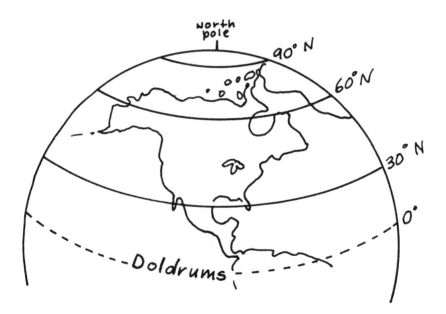

Answer

Think!

• The hot air rises above the doldrums, moves toward the North Pole, cools, and sinks toward the earth at latitude 30°N. Thus:

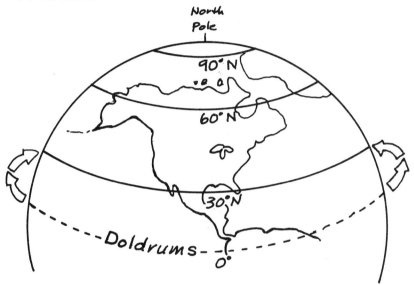

Exercises

The air rising from the doldrums is generally sinking toward the earth at latitudes 30°N and 30°S. This area often has no steady surface winds. When ships traveling to the New World became stranded here, the horses on board could no longer be supported and were thrown overboard to save water and supplies. These latitudes came to be known as the **horse latitudes**.

1. Trace the diagram of the globe and label these parts:

  • Doldrums.

  • Horse latitudes.

- North Pole.

- South Pole.

2. On your diagram of the globe, use arrows to show the cyclic air flow between the doldrums and the horse latitudes.

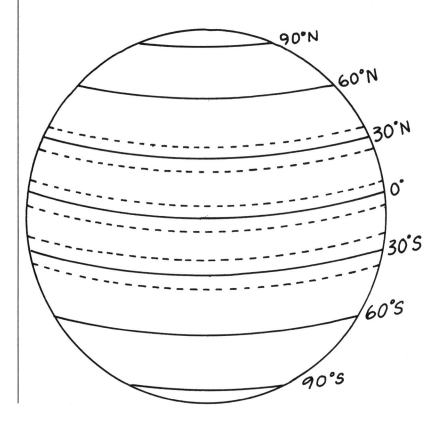

Activity: CONVECTION CURRENTS

Purpose To simulate the movement of air currents due to
convection (the movement of heat through gases and liquids).

Materials 4 to 5 ice cubes
2 1-quart (1-liter) large-mouth jars
cold tap water
baby food jar
warm tap water
spoon
green food coloring
4-inch (10-cm) square of aluminum foil
rubber band
pencil
timer

Procedure

1. Place the ice cubes in one of the jars. Fill the jar with the
   cold water.

2. Fill the baby food jar to overflowing with the warm water. Stir in 10 drops of the food coloring.

3. Cover the mouth of the baby food jar with the foil and
   secure it with the rubberband.

4. Stand the baby food jar inside the second quart (liter) jar.

5. Remove the unmelted ice cubes from the first jar and
   pour the chilled water into the second jar, filling it three-
   fourths full.

6. Use the point of the pencil to make one small hole
   slightly off center in the foil.

7. From the side, observe the contents of the jar for about five seconds.

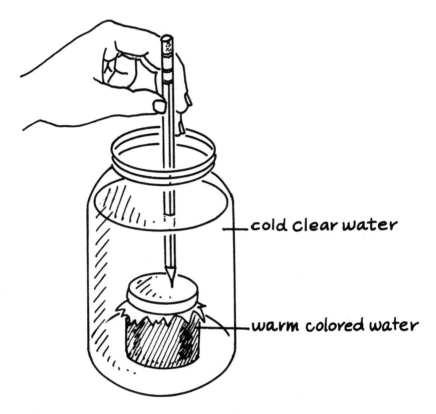

cold clear water

warm colored water

8. Make a second hole in the foil.

9. Observe the contents again.

10. Continue to observe the contents every five minutes for 20 minutes.

Results   Nothing happens with only one hole in the aluminum foil, but with two holes a stream of green water rises and moves along the surface of the cold water. After a while, the streams of green water start sinking.

Why?   Water molecules, like air or any form of matter, are closer together when cold and farther apart when hot. Thus, the clear cold water weighs more than the colored warm water because its molecules are more densely packed together. When there is only one hole in the foil, the lighter warm water is prevented from rising because of the pressure of the heavier cold water above it. The cold water cannot enter through the hole in the foil because the baby food jar is filled with water. Adding a second hole allows the cold water to sink into the jar, pushing out of its way the warm water, which rises to the top. This rising and sinking movement of liquids or gases due to differences in temperature is called **convection currents**. Air currents move around the earth as the warm air near the equator rises and flows up toward the poles. The cold polar air sinks and flows down toward the equator.

Solution to Exercises

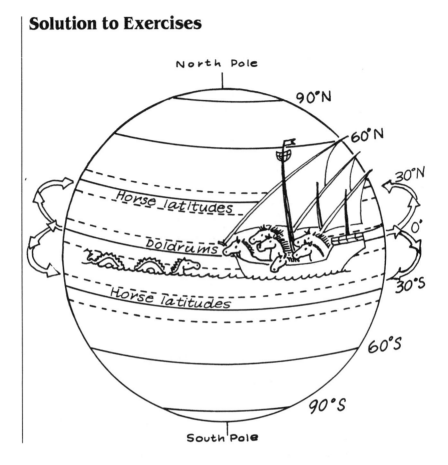

17
Water and Climate
Study the Effect of Water on Climate

What You Need to Know

How close an area of land is to water affects its climate. The interior of a continent is usually hotter in the summer and colder in the winter than its coastline because land cools and heats faster than water. Because water changes temperature more slowly, the land close to it has a more moderate climate. Water from lakes, streams, and oceans not only affects temperature, but also provides a source of moisture for **precipitation** (rain, snow, hail, and sleet).

Ocean currents are large streams of ocean water flowing in the same direction. Because of the effect of winds, the earth's rotation, and the position of continents, currents generally flow clockwise in the Northern Hemisphere and counterclockwise in the Southern Hemisphere. Ocean currents transport vast amounts of water from one place to another. The difference in the temperature of the currents results in the movement of warm equatorial waters toward the poles and cool polar waters toward the equator.

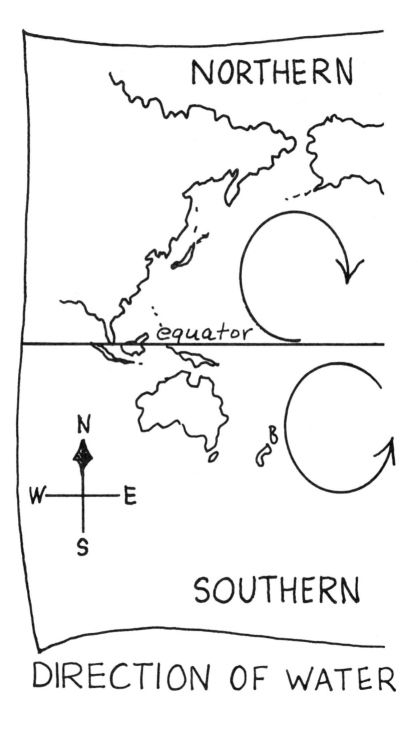

NORTHERN

equator

N
W — E
S

SOUTHERN

DIRECTION OF WATER

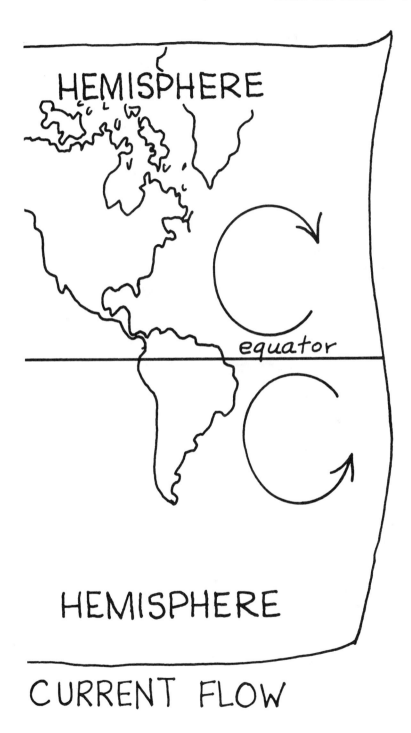

HEMISPHERE

equator

HEMISPHERE

CURRENT FLOW

Let's Think It Through

Use the map of Ocean Currents 1 to answer the following questions:

1. Is the Brazil Current a warm or cold current?

2. Which should have a milder climate, the western coast of Norway or the eastern coast of Greenland?

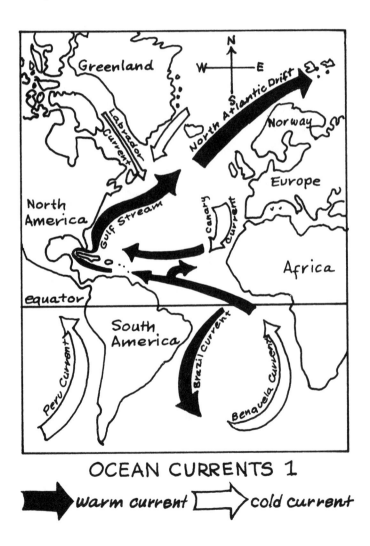

OCEAN CURRENTS 1

warm current ⬌ cold current

Answers

1. *Think!*

- Is the line for the Brazil Current solid or an open outline? Solid.

- Look at the map legend. What type of current does a solid line indicate? A warm current.

The Brazil Current is warm.

2. *Think!*

- Coastlines with warm ocean currents have warm, mild climates. Which of the areas has a warm ocean current flowing along its coast? Norway.

The western coast of Norway has a milder climate than the eastern coast of Greenland.

NOTE: Despite its northerly location, Norway has relatively warm winters due to the influence of the warm Gulf Stream that originates near the equator and becomes the North Atlantic Drift.

Exercises

1. Generally warm currents move north or south away from the equator, while cold currents usually move toward the equator. Use this information to complete the legend showing cold and warm currents for the Ocean Currents 2 map.

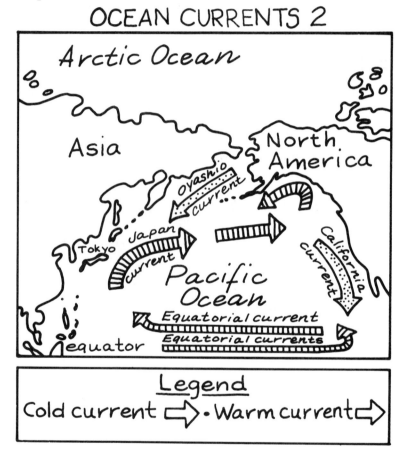

OCEAN CURRENTS 2

2. The United Kingdom and Labrador are in the same latitude. Use the map of currents in this area to determine
which of these land areas has the milder climate.

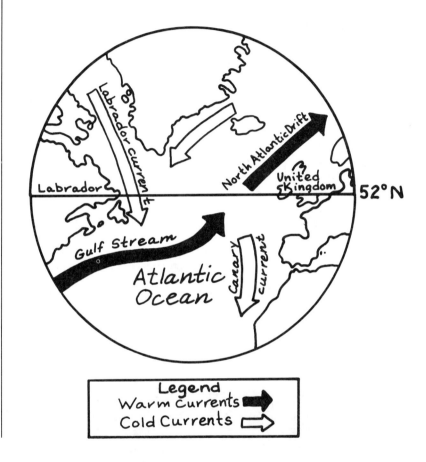

Activity: LAND AND SEA BREEZES

Purpose To determine the cause of land and sea breezes.

Materials 2 thermometers
2 glasses large enough to hold the thermometers
soil
cold tap water
desk lamp
timer

Procedure

1. Stand a thermometer in each glass.

2. Add enough soil to one of the glasses to barely cover the bulb of the thermometer.

3. Add an equal amount of water to the second glass.

4. Set the glasses together on a table away from direct sunlight.

5. After five minutes, read and record the temperature on each thermometer.

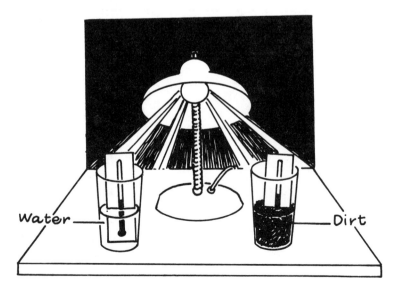

6. Position the lamp so that the light hits both glasses evenly.

7. After two hours, read and record the temperature on each thermometer.

8. Turn the lamp off.

9. Wait two hours and read and record the temperature on each thermometer again.

Results The temperature of the soil rises faster than the water. The soil also cools faster than the water.

Why? The difference in the time it takes the soil and water to change temperature can be used to explain the difference in the direction of day and night breezes along a coastline. During the day, even though the sun shines equally on the land and

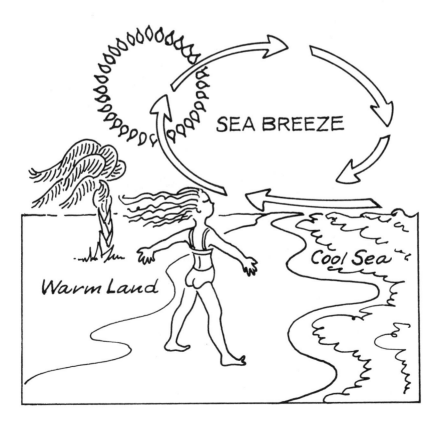

water, the land heats more quickly than the water. The warmer air above the land rises, and the cooler air above the water rushes inland to take its place. This cool breeze blowing from the water toward the land during the day is called a **sea breeze**. At night the land cools faster than the water. The warmer air above the water rises, and the cooler air from the land rushes out to sea. This cool night breeze is called a **land breeze**.

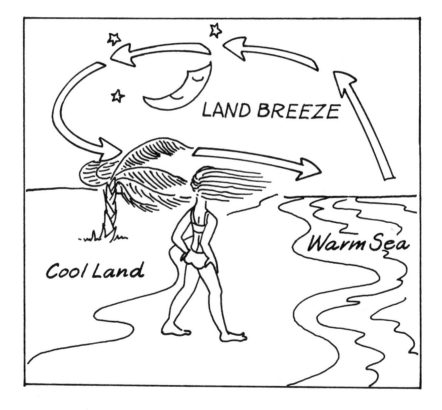

Solutions to Exercises

1.

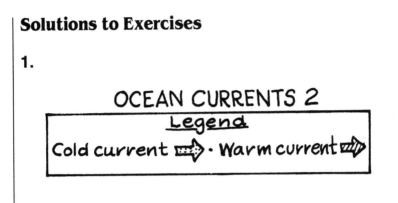

2. The United Kingdom has a more moderate climate than Labrador because of the warm ocean current, the North Atlantic Drift.

18

Climate Regions

Determine How a Region's Location and Its Landforms Affect Its Climate

What You Need to Know

Early in the 20th century, Vladimir Köppen, a German **botanist** (scientist who studies plants) and **climatologist** (scientist who studies climate), observed the relationship between the types of plants that grow in a specific climate and the area's average measures of temperature and precipitation. He used his observations to draw boundary lines on a world map that has been used to divide the earth into six general climate regions briefly described as follows:

1. **Tropical climate:** Hot and steamy with an abundance of plant growth in the rain forest. In the savanas it is wet only half the year and dry the other half.

2. **Dry climate:** Hot, desert conditions with little precipitation.

3. **Mild climate:** Moderate with few extremes of temperature or precipitation.

4. **Continental climate:** Widely variable temperatures and precipitation.

5. **Polar climate:** Long, frigid winters, with brief summers in some areas lasting from one to two months, little

precipitation, with polar ice melting in summer to wet the ground for plant growth.

6. **High-altitude climate:** Widely variable temperatures and precipitation depending on the altitude and latitude of its landforms.

Climate Region Chart

Climate	Characteristics
1. Tropical	
2. Dry	
3. Mild	
4. Continental	
5. Polar	
6. High altitude	

The six climate regions do not have boundaries where one climate suddenly ends and another begins. Rather, the climates usually change gradually. If a landform such as a mountain range near a large body of water divides the region, then one side of the mountain can be cool and wet and support plant growth, while the opposite side is a desert with a warm, dry climate and minimal plant life. As winds blow across water, they pick up moisture, then rise and pass over the mountain. The air cools and the moisture precipitates as rain or snow. The precipitation in the diagram is falling on the mountain's **windward side** (side facing the wind), and a dry wind blows over and onto the land on its **leeward side** (side protected from the wind).

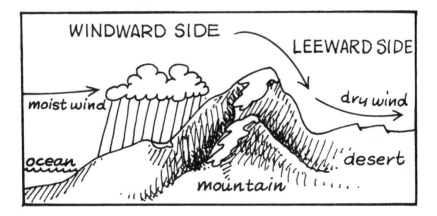

Let's Think It Through

Use the African Climate Regions map to determine the approximate latitude range for the following climates:

1. Tropical climate.

2. Dry climate.

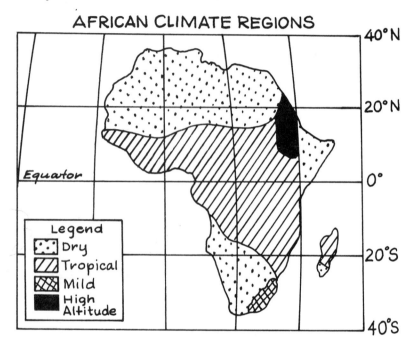

Answers

1. *Think!*

- Look at the map legend. What pattern indicates a tropical climates? Stripes.

- Between which two latitudes do most of the striped areas appear?

Most of the tropical climate is between latitudes 20°N and 20°S.

2. *Think!*

- What legend pattern represents a dry climate? Dots.

- Between which two latitudes do most of the dotted areas appear?

Most of the dry climate is between latitudes 40°N and 0° (equator).

Exercises

Generally, temperatures decrease as one travels away from the equator toward the poles. Therefore, the earth can be divided into three latitude zones: tropical, middle, and polar. Use the Latitude Zones map to determine the latitude range for the following zones:

1. Tropics.

2. Middle latitude.

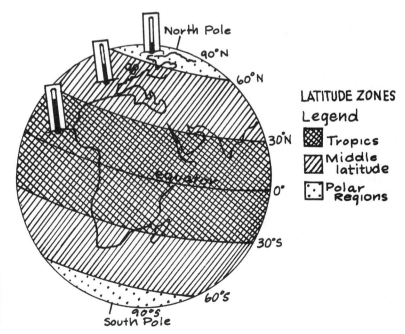

Activity: THE WATER CYCLE

Purpose To demonstrate the movement of water between the earth and the air.

Materials 1 cup (250 ml) soil
2-quart (2-liter) glass bowl
½ cup (125 ml) tap water
sheet of transparent plastic food wrap large
   enough to cover the bowl
gooseneck desk lamp
timer
ice cube
zip-lock plastic bag

Procedure

1. Pour the soil into the bowl and make it as level as possible.

2. Pour the water over the surface of the soil.

3. Cover the bowl with the food wrap, making sure it is tightly sealed.

4. Place the bowl on a table near the lamp.

5. Position the lamp so that the light is about 6 inches (15 cm) away from the side of the bowl.

6. After 10 minutes, place the ice cube in the bag and gently rub it over the surface of the plastic cover. While doing this, observe the appearance of the cover.

7. Remove the bag of ice and gently run your finger across the surface of the cover.

Results Rubbing the plastic with the ice causes the plastic to change from clear to cloudy. Running your finger over the plastic cover reveals that it is dry on the outside. (The bag keeps the melting ice from wetting the cover so you can prove it is dry.)

Why? The cover's cloudy appearance is due to the formation of moisture on the underside. The bowl of damp soil simulates the movement of water between the earth and the air. This movement of water is called the **water cycle**. One stage in the water cycle is the **evaporation** of water from the land, or the changing of a liquid to a vapor as it enters the air. This stage requires an increase in the liquid's temperature by the sun, the lamp in this experiment. Not only does the liquid from bodies of water such as oceans, lakes, and streams evaporate, but also does the water in soil, laundry, and anything else that is wet.

Once in the air, the water vapor cools and changes back to a liquid. This change from vapor to liquid is called **condensation**. It is what makes the plastic appear cloudy. This stage requires a decrease in the vapor's temperature, such as at nightfall, simulated by the ice cube. In nature, clouds form when water condenses in the cooler upper atmosphere. The liquid water in the clouds returns to the earth as precipitation, which can evaporate, starting the water cycle again.

Solutions to Exercises

1. *Think!*

- Look at the map legend. Which pattern indicates the tropical zone? Crosshatched.

- Between which two latitudes is the shaded area?

The tropics are between latitudes 30°N and 30°S.

2. *Think!*

- Which legend pattern represents the middle latitude? Striped.

- Between which latitudes do the striped areas appear?

There are two middle latitude regions: one between latitudes 30°N and 60°N, and one between latitudes 30°S and 60°S.

19

Waters and Lands of the Earth

Identify and Locate the Seven Continents and Four Oceans of the World

What You Need to Know

Astronauts looking down at the earth from space see a sphere that looks like a huge, beautiful, blue-and-white marble. Only about one-fourth of the earth's surface is land. The remaining, approximately three-fourths of the surface, is covered with water. The largest bodies of water are the **oceans**, which are spread unevenly over the earth. Most of the land on the earth is in the Northern Hemisphere, while most of the Southern Hemisphere is water.

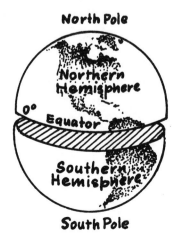

177

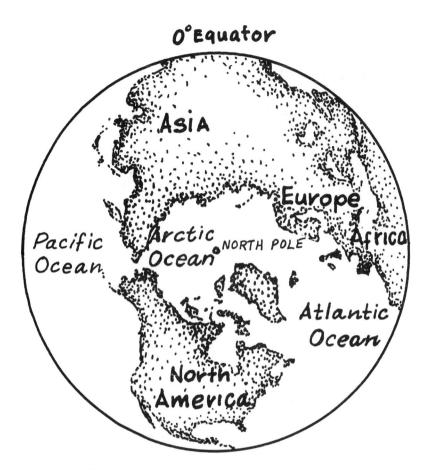

VIEW OF NORTHERN HEMISPHERE

Note: Compare these bird's-eye views of the earth with the globe on pages 180–181.

VIEW OF SOUTHERN HEMISPHERE

The oceans are not actually separate bodies of water, but one great ocean with the continents floating in it like islands. This great ocean is divided by scientists into four parts, which in order of size from largest to smallest are the Pacific Ocean, Atlantic Ocean, Indian Ocean, and Arctic Ocean. The largest and deepest ocean is the Pacific, with a total area approximately equal to the combined areas of the three other oceans. The **seas** are also large bodies of water, but they are smaller than oceans and may or may not be part of an ocean.

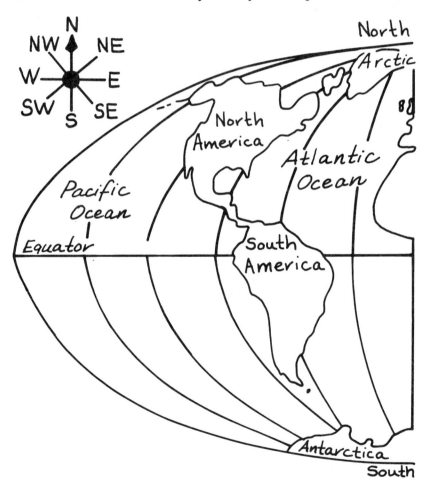

WORLD MAP OF CONTINENTS AND OCEANS

The land on the surface of the earth is divided into six major landmasses called **continents**: North America, South America, Africa, Australia, Antarctica, and Eurasia. However, it is usually said that there are seven continents, since the largest landmass (Eurasia), is divided into two continents (Europe and Asia).

Let's Think It Through

Use the World Map of Continents and Oceans to answer the following questions:

1. Which continent is due south of Europe?

2. Which two continents are directly west of the Atlantic Ocean?

Answers

1. *Think!*

- Find Europe on the map. Which direction is south? Straight down toward the bottom of the page.

- What is the first continent directly below Europe?

Africa is due south of Europe.

2. *Think!*

- Which direction is west? Toward the left.

- Find the Atlantic Ocean. Which two continents are to the left of it?

North American and South America are west of the Atlantic Ocean.

Exercises

1. Use map A to answer the following question. Imagine yourself standing in the state of Florida. If you travel south, which sea would you reach first?

2. Use map B to answer the following question. Imagine yourself standing directly over the South Pole in the continent of Antarctica. Which of the continents are north of where you are standing?

MAP A.

Beaufort Sea

Bering Sea

N. America

Atlantic Ocean

Florida

Caribbean Sea

Pacific Ocean

N

W — E

S

S. America

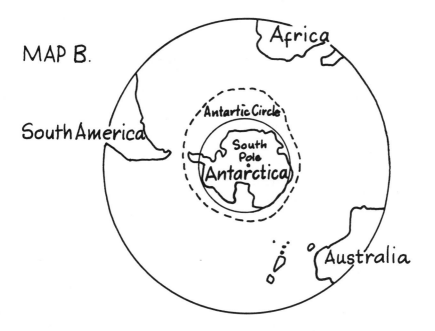

MAP B.

Africa

South America

Antartic Circle

South Pole

Antarctica

Australia

Activity: INNER OVERCOATS

Purpose To demonstrate how the location of a continent affects its animal life.

Materials 1 tablespoon (15 ml) shortening
2 thermometers
2 cotton balls
2 cups
freezer
timer

Procedure

1. Mold the shortening around the bulb of one thermometer.

2. Pull the fibers of one cotton ball apart and wrap them around the shortening.

3. Stand the first thermometer in one of the cups.

4. Wrap the second thermometer's bulb only with the fibers of the second cotton ball.

5. Stand the second thermometer in the second cup.

6. Read and record the temperature shown on each thermometer.

7. Place the cups and their thermometers in the freezer and shut the door.

8. Take temperature readings every five minutes until 20 minutes have passed.

shortening
and
cotton

cotton
only

Results   In 20 minutes, the readings on the thermometer covered with shortening and cotton changed less than the temperature on the thermometer covered only with cotton.

Why?   Continents located near the equator receive more direct sunlight and have warmer climates. The farther a continent is from the equator, the colder its climate. Penguins can survive in Antarctica, the southernmost and coldest continent, because the fat layer under their skin acts like an **insulator** (material that slows down the transfer of heat energy). The shortening in the experiment, like the fat layer of the penguin, also acts as an insulator. This "inner overcoat" slows down the heat flow away from the warm inner body of the animal to the cold air outside the body. Fat layers plus their outer feathers **adapt** (make suitable for survival) the penguin to the frigid conditions of Antarctica. If placed on a continent located closer to the equator, such as Australia, the penguin would be most uncomfortable and probably die. The animals of Australia are adapted to its warm climate and would not survive the conditions of Antarctica because they do not have inner overcoats.

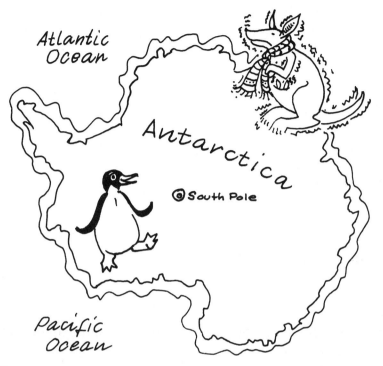

Solutions to Exercises

1. *Think!*

- On map A, which direction is south? Toward the bottom of the page.

- Locate Florida and trace with your finger a southward path until it touches the sea.

The Caribbean Sea is the first sea south of Florida.

2. *Think!*

- Standing at the South Pole is like standing on the top of a huge ball. Which direction of travel is north of the South Pole? All directions.

- Which continents in map B are north of the South Pole?

South America, Africa, and Australia.

20
People, Population, and Location

Looking at World Population and How It Has Changed

What You Need to Know

The number of people living on the earth can be approximated because most of the countries of the world take an official count of their **population** (number of people living in an area such as a city) known as a **census**. Countries that do not take an official census provide an **estimate** (guess based on facts) of their population. Using the population figures from each country of the world, the United Nations proclaimed that Matej Gaspar, a boy born in Zagreb, Yugoslavia, on Saturday, July 11, 1987, became the world's 5 billionth inhabitant. This number increases daily as more babies are born around the world.

You, your family and friends, and the people that live around you are a part of the more than 5 billion (5,000,000,000) people that make up the earth's population, which is **distributed** (spread out) over the earth in different regions. The major factors that influence where people live is the availability of food and fresh water needed for survival. The **population density** (average number of people living in a square area) increases in areas where these needs can be easily met.

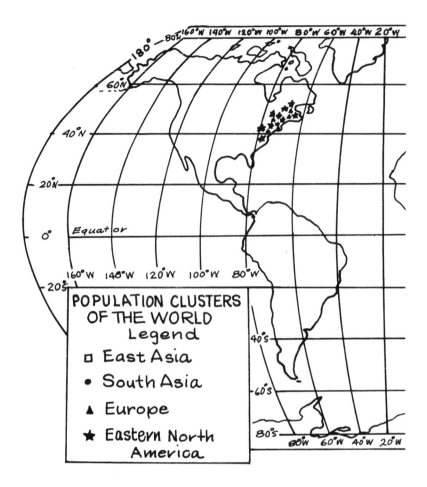

Some of the geographical influences that attract people to specific locations are favorable climates, fertile land for farming, and nearness to rivers or the ocean. The waterways provide food and a means of transportation, as well as a means of defense for the **community** (a group of people who live near each other). A study of the distribution of the earth's population will reveal that some communities of people live in very unfavorable geographic regions. To survive, these people make changes to their environment or live a nomadic life-style. **Nomads** are people who have no fixed location, but move from one place to another in search of food and water. Because of

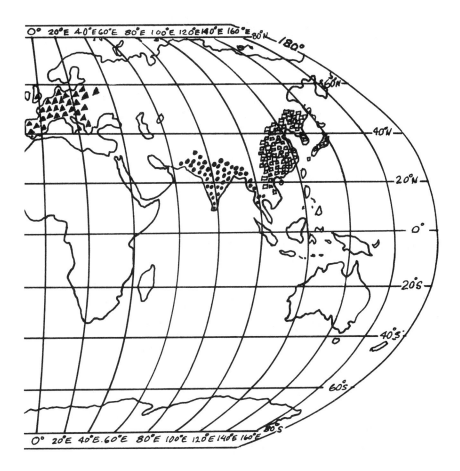

the advanced technological era in which we live, communities can now choose to live in a geographic area that in the past would have been considered unfavorable.

Basically, much of the earth's inhabitants can be divided into four main population clusters or groups:

1. *East Asia:* More than one-fourth of the people on the earth live in this cluster, which includes Korea, Taiwan, Japan, Viet Nam, and China.

2. *South Asia:* This is the second largest populated area on earth. India, Nepal, Sri Lanka, Pakistan, and Bangladesh are part of this cluster.

3. *Europe:* This is the third largest cluster and includes many highly populated countries, some of the largest being Great Britain, France, Germany, and Italy.

4. *Eastern North America:* This is the smallest of the four clusters and covers an area along the east coast of the continent.

Let's Think It Through

The population of the earth changed very slowly from its beginning until about A.D. 1700, probably because of disease, war, and famine. Improvements in food production and medical discoveries that helped people live longer caused the earth's population to increase.

Use the World Population Growth chart to answer these questions:

1. Between which two dates did the earth's population remain **stable** (unchanged)?

WORLD POPULATION GROWTH

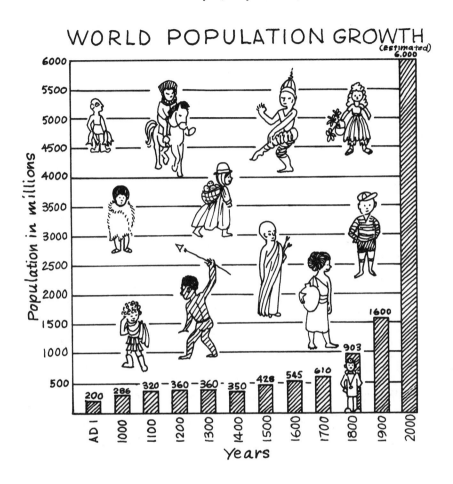

2. How many more people inhabited the earth in 1600 than in 1500?

3. Between which two consecutive dates does the population increase the most?

Answers

1. *Think!*

- Which two consecutive dates on the charts have the same population?

The earth's population remained stable between 1200 and 1300.

2. *Think!*

- What was the population of the earth in 1600? It was 545 million. What was the population in 1500? It was 428 million.

- What is the difference between these numbers?

  545 million − 428 million = 117 million

There were 117 million more people in 1600 than in 1500.

3. *Think!*

- Which two consecutive dates show the greatest difference in the height of their bars on the graph?

The population increases most between 1900 and 2000.

Exercises

1. According to the European Population Growth chart, how many more people are estimated to inhabit Europe in the year 2000 than lived there in 1900?

2. The bubonic plague, known as the Black Death, killed many people in Europe. According to the chart, between what dates did this plague most likely occur?

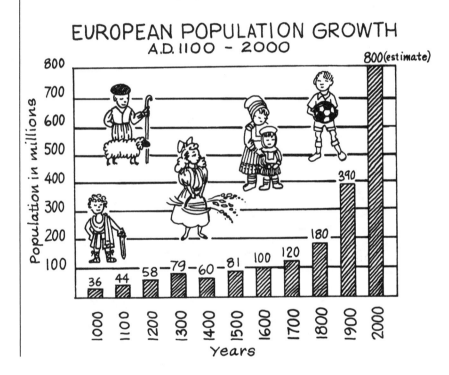

EUROPEAN POPULATION GROWTH
A.D. 1100 - 2000

Activity: PAPER DOLL PEOPLE

Purpose   To demonstrate population density.

Materials   six 3-by-5-inch (7.5-by-12.5-cm) unruled index
   cards
   marking pen
   scissors
   sheet of typing paper
   ruler

Procedure

1. Fold one index card in half so that the short edges meet.

2. Fold each short edge back toward the fold, into an accordion shape.

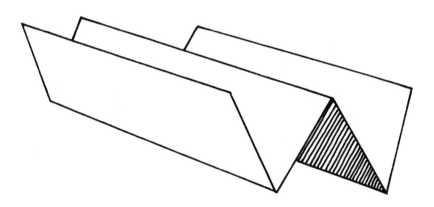

3. Draw dashed lines on one side of the folded card, as on diagram taking note of the position of the folded and open edges in the diagram.

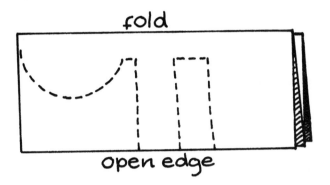

4. Cut the folded card along the dashed lines.

5. Unfold the card and draw faces, hair, and clothes on the two paper dolls.

6. Fold along the line indicated in the diagram to make a stand for the dolls.

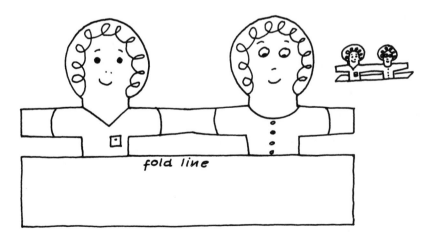

7. Repeat the procedure to construct 5 more sets of paper dolls.

8. Fold the typing paper in half twice to form four square areas.

9. Open the folded paper and draw lines along the creases in the paper.

10. Label the cities and their populations as shown in the diagram. Note that each set of paper dolls represents 20,000 people.

11. Place three sets of dolls in the square for the city of Fort Sara.

12. Place one set in each square for the cities of Sabrinaville, Alicia Springs, and Mount Stephanie.

Results   The population density of Fort Sara is three times as large as that of the neighboring cities of Sabrinaville, Mount Stephanie, and Alicia Springs.

Why?   A community is defined by its population density and the services it provides. From the least to the most densely populated, the four types of communities are as follows:

1. A **hamlet** has a small group of homes and possibly a gas station and a general store.

2. A **village** has more people than a hamlet, but less than a town and provides services such as a post office, a church, and maybe a restaurant.

3. A **town** has such services as specialty stores.

4. A **city** has the most people and the most public services.

Cities are usually surrounded by smaller towns, villages, and/ or hamlets. The smaller communities outside a city are called **suburbs**. A city and its surrounding suburbs is called a **metropolitan area**. Fort Sara with its large population density is a city surrounded by the suburban communities of Mount Stephanie, Sabrinaville, and Alicia Springs. Together these communities are an example of a metropolitan area. When metropolitan areas grow into each other, they become a **megalopolis**.

Solutions to Exercises

1. *Think!*

- What is the estimated population of Europe for the year 2000? It is 800 million.

- What was the population in 1900? It was 390 million.

- What is the difference between these numbers?

    800 million − 390 million = 410 million

In the year 2000, 410 million more people will inhabit Europe than in 1900.

2. *Think!*

- At what date is the population less than the preceding date? In 1400. This indicates that the deathrate was more than the birthrate between 1300 and 1400.

The bubonic plague probably occurred between 1300 and 1400.

NOTE: *History records that the bubonic plague killed about one-third of the entire population of Europe between 1348 and 1370.*

Glossary

Adapt: To make suitable for survival.

Air: A mixture of gases—composed mostly of nitrogen, oxygen, carbon dioxide, and water vapor.

Altitude: The height of an object.

Angle of magnetic declination: (See **Variation**.)

Astronomer: A scientist who studies the stars and other objects in space.

Autumnal equinox: The point through which the sun passes on the first day of autumn (September 23 in the Northern Hemisphere).

Botanist: A scientist who studies plants.

Cartographer: A mapmaker.

Census: An official count of the population of a given area.

City: The largest form of community, having a large population and many public services.

Climate: The pattern of weather that one region has over a long period of time.

Climatologist: A scientist who studies climate.

Community: A group of people who live near each other as well as the place they live; defined by its population density and services it provides; hamlet, village, town, or city.

Compass: An instrument used to determine directions by means of a free-swinging magnetic needle that always points to the magnetic north.

Compass rose: An instrument used to measure directions in degrees.

Condensation: The stage in the water cycle when a vapor changes to a liquid; requires a decrease in energy.

Continent: One of six major landmasses on the earth (North America, South America, Africa, Australia, Antarctica, and Eurasia/Europe and Asia).

Continental climate: A climate characterized by widely variable temperatures and precipitation.

Continental shelf: The part of the ocean floor starting at the shoreline of a continent and going outward to sea; varies in width from almost nothing to about 1,000 miles (1,600 km), averaging about 41 miles (66 km).

Contour interval: The altitude change between contour lines; represents grade.

Contour lines: Irregular loops on a topographic map that connect points of equal elevation or depth.

Convection: The movement of heat through gases and liquids.

Convection currents: The up-and-down movement of liquids or gases due to differences in temperature.

Coordinate: The degree and direction of a longitude or latitude line.

Coriolis effect: The tendency of winds and water to bend due to the earth's rotation.

Cyclone: A wind blowing in a circle.

Distributed: Spread out.

Doldrums: Region of little surface wind near the equator.

Dry climate: A climate characterized by hot, desert conditions and little precipitation.

Echo time: The time it takes for sound waves to travel in a straight path, reflect off an object, and return.

Elevation: The altitude of the land above a reference point, usually sea level.

Equator: An imaginary line circling the earth at latitude 0°; the starting point for measuring distances north or south on a map or globe.

Estimate: A guess based on facts.

Evaporation: The stage in the water cycle when a liquid changes to a vapor; requires an increase in energy.

Eye of the storm: The calm area of clear skies in the center of a tropical cyclone.

Geographic north pole: The true north pole of the earth; located at latitude 90°N; points toward Polaris.

Geography: A branch of science that encompasses all aspects of the earth's physical features and inhabitants.

Gores: Long, elliptical, pointed sections made by peeling off the "skin" of a sphere; used to form the flat surface of a map of the globe.

Grade: The steepness of an elevation.

Hamlet: A community having a small group of homes and few if any public services.

High-altitude climate: A climate characterized by widely variable temperature and precipitation depending on the altitude and latitude of its landforms.

Horse latitudes: Region of little surface wind at latitudes 30°N and 30°S.

Hurricane: A tropical cyclone with winds of 74 miles per hour (118 kmph) or more.

Insulator: Any material that slows down the transfer of heat energy.

International date line: An imaginary line located at longitude 180°; a traveler crossing this line finds that the time remains the same, but the date changes.

Land breeze: A cool breeze blowing from the land toward the water during the night.

Latitude: The imaginary lines circling the globe in an east-west direction; also called parallel of latitude.

Leeward side: The side protected from the wind.

Legend: A key for decoding symbols on a map.

Longitude: Imaginary lines circling the globe in a north-south direction. Measured in degrees east or west of the prime meridian; also called meridians of longitude.

Magnetic north pole: The point on the earth's surface toward which the north poles of all magnets are attracted; located at about latitude 75°N and longitude 101°W.

Map projection: The transferring of information about the earth's surface to a flat map.

Megalopolis: The area produced when metropolitan areas grow into each other.

Mercator projection map: A flat drawing of the earth that accurately gives shapes for small areas, but is not an equal-area projection, and exaggerates the areas of places that lie a great distance from the equator.

Meridians of longitude: (See **Longitude**.)

Mesa: A hill with a flat top and at least one side that is a steep cliff.

Meteorologist: A scientist who studies weather patterns.

Metropolitan area: A city and its surrounding suburbs.

Mild climate: A moderate climate that has few extremes of temperature or precipitation.

Nomads: People who have no fixed location, but move from one place to another in search of food and water.

Northern Hemisphere: The region of the earth north of the equator.

Ocean: One of the large bodies of water that is part of the great ocean, as the Pacific Ocean.

Ocean currents: Large streams of ocean water flowing in the same direction.

Orbit: The path of a celestial body, such as a planet, around the sun.

Pace: One giant step, used for measuring distances.

Parallels of latitude: (See **Latitude**.)

Planet: Greek word meaning wanderer; one of the celestial bodies that moves around the sun.

Polar climate: A climate characterized by long frigid winters, with brief summers in some areas lasting from one to two months, little precipitation, with polar ice melting in summer to wet the ground for plant growth.

Polaris: The North Star; used by early explorers in navigation because its position above the horizon changes depending on where one is; above the earth's geographic north pole.

Population: The number of people living in an area such as a city.

Population density: The average number of people living in a square area.

Precipitation: Falling moisture from clouds, such as rain, snow, hail, sleet, etc.; a stage in the water cycle.

Prime meridian: An imaginary line at longitude 0° that runs through Greenwich, London; the starting point for measuring distances east or west on a map or globe.

Revolution: The movement of one object around another; the movement of the earth and other celestial bodies around the sun.

Rotation: The spinning movement of an object, such as the earth on its axis.

Scale: A key on a map that uses a small measure to represent a larger area on the earth.

Sea: A large body of water smaller than an ocean that may or may not be part of an ocean.

Sea breeze: A cool breeze blowing from the water toward the land during the day.

Solar system: A group of celestial bodies revolving around the sun.

Sonar device: An instrument used for sending ultrasonic waves.

Southern Hemisphere: The region of the earth south of the equator.

Sphere: An object shaped like a ball.

Stable: Unchanged.

Suburbs: The smaller communities outside a city.

Summer solstice: The point through which the sun passes on the first day of summer (June 22 in the Northern Hemisphere).

Topographic map: A map that indicates the shape and elevation of features of the earth's surface, such as mountains, lakes, rivers, roads, and cities.

Town: A community that is between a city and a village in population and availability of public services.

Tropic of Cancer: Latitude 23½°N.

Tropic of Capricorn: Latitude 23½°S.

Tropical climate: Hot and steamy with an abundance of plant growth in the rain forest. In the savanas it is wet only half the year and dry the other half.

Tropical depression: A tropical cyclone with a wind speed of less than 39 miles per hour (62 kmph).

Tropical storm: A tropical cyclone with a wind speed of 39–73 miles per hour (62–116 kmph).

Ultrasonic waves: High-frequency sound waves.

Variation: The angle of difference between the direction toward geographic north and magnetic north from a given point on the earth; the angle of magnetic declination.

Vernal equinox: The point through which the sun passes on the first day of spring (March 21 in the Northern Hemisphere).

Village: A community having more population and public services than a hamlet, but fewer of these than a town.

Water cycle: The movement of water between the earth and the air in three stages—evaporation, condensation, and precipitation.

Wind: The motion caused by the movement of air.

Windward side: The side facing the wind.

Winter solstice: The point through which the sun passes on the first day of winter (December 22 in the Northern Hemisphere).

Index

Get these fun and exciting books by Janice VanCleave at your local bookstore, call toll-free 1-800-225-5945 or visit our Web site at: www.wiley.com/children/

Janice VanCleave's Science for Every Kid Series

____Astronomy	53573-7	$12.95 US / 15.95 CAN
____Biology	50381-9	$11.95 US / 15.95 CAN
____Chemistry	62085-8	$11.95 US / 15.95 CAN
____Constellations	15979-4	$12.95 US / 15.95 CAN
____Dinosaurs	30812-9	$10.95 US / 15.95 CAN
____Earth Science	53010-7	$12.95 US / 15.95 CAN
____Ecology	10086-2	$10.95 US / 15.95 CAN
____Geography	59842-9	$12.95 US / 19.95 CAN
____Geometry	31141-3	$11.95 US / 15.95 CAN
____Human Body	02408-2	$12.95 US / 15.95 CAN
____Math	54265-2	$12.95 US / 15.95 CAN
____Oceans	12453-2	$12.95 US / 15.95 CAN
____Physics	52505-7	$12.95 US / 15.95 CAN

Janice VanCleave's Spectacular Science Projects Series

____Animals	55052-3	$10.95 US / 12.95 CAN
____Earthquakes	57107-5	$10.95 US / 12.95 CAN
____Electricity	31010-7	$10.95 US / 12.95 CAN
____Gravity	55050-7	$10.95 US / 12.95 CAN
____Insects & Spiders	16396-1	$10.95 US / 15.50 CAN
____Machines	57108-3	$10.95 US / 12.95 CAN
____Magnets	57106-7	$10.95 US / 12.95 CAN
____Microscopes & Magnifying Lenses	58956-X	$10.95 US / 12.95 CAN
____Molecules	55054-X	$10.95 US / 12.95 CAN
____Plants	14687-0	$10.95 US / 12.95 CAN
____Rocks & Minerals	10269-5	$10.95 US / 12.95 CAN
____Volcanoes	30811-0	$10.95 US / 12.95 CAN
____Weather	03231-X	$10.95 US / 12.95 CAN

Janice VanCleave's Science Bonanzas Series

____200 Gooey, Slippery, Slimy, Weird & Fun Experiments
        57921-1 $12.95 US / 16.95 CAN

____201 Awesome, Magical, Bizarre & Incredible Experiments
        31011-5 $12.95 US / 16.95 CAN

____202 Oozing, Bubbling, Dripping & Bouncing Experiments
        14025-2 $12.95 US / 16.95 CAN

Janice VanCleave's Play and Find Out About Science Series

____Play and Find Out About the Human Body
        12935-6 $12.95 US / 18.50 CAN

____Play and Find Out About Nature
        12940-2 $12.95 US / 16.95 CAN

____Play and Find Out About Math
        12938-0 $12.95 US / 18.50 CAN

____Play and Find Out About Science
        12941-0 $12.95 US / 16.95 CAN

Janice VanCleave's Guide to the Best Science Fair Projects

____Guide to the Best Science Fair Projects
        14802-4 $14.95 US / 19.95 CAN

Janice VanCleave's A+ Projects for Young Adults Series

____Biology	58628-5	$12.95 US / 17.95 CAN
____Chemistry	58630-7	$12.95 US / 17.95 CAN

Prices subject to change without notice.